To: Jo

Great memories

VIEWS FROM THE PULPIT

(Things Observed and Learned

in the Pastoral Ministry)

John W. Krueger

John Krueger

xulon
PRESS

Copyright © 2012 by John W. Krueger

Views from the Pulpit
by John W. Krueger

Printed in the United States of America

ISBN 9781622308088

All rights reserved solely by the author. The author guarantees all contents are original and do not infringe upon the legal rights of any other person or work. No part of this book may be reproduced in any form without the permission of the author. The views expressed in this book are not necessarily those of the publisher.

Unless otherwise indicated, Bible quotations are taken from the New International Version, (NIV). Copyright © 1984 by Zondervan Publishers.

www.xulonpress.com

Dedicated to the congregations of
Faith
St. John's
Christ
Grace
Gethsemane

Introduction

In an advanced preaching class I took at Fuller Seminary in Pasadena, the professor emphasized that it was important that the congregation understand exactly what the point of the message is. He then went on to tell us that indeed one great preacher simply told the congregation in the introduction what the sermon was going to be about. So here goes.

This book is about things I have observed and about things I have learned in the pastoral ministry. It is about a whole range of things—people, events, ideas, places, the Body of Christ and other things that come to mind.

In my 36 years of full time ministry I had the privilege of serving 5 congregations, over 5,000 people, and the real joy (the best part) of bringing more than 500 people into the church (and some of them into the Church) through adult instruction and Confirmation. As all of this happened I saw a lot, and I learned a lot about life, about ministry, about various things which I want to share, and about the immeasurable love of God through our Lord Jesus Christ and the power and insight of the Holy Spirit.

Having said that, of course I am also thankful to Nancy and our family, and to the many people mentioned in this book (not their real names) and to many others along the way.

Hope you like it!

TABLE OF CONTENTS

Part One

God works in so many ways in the lives of individual people. The first section of this book simply talks about people I have known along the way. The stories are of interest, not because they are unique, but simply because they show the varied interactions of people with each other and with God.

Chapter One

People of Note

Will

I had a call. It was to a town I had never heard of. We had a new baby; we had been in our new house for only 6 months. I hung up the phone and said, "Nancy, we might have to move." I had not put my name out for a call, neither had I had any contact with my district president, nor the district president of the calling congregation. But God knew. The vacancy pastor was a friend of a pastor who knew me. The one who knew me told the vacancy pastor, "While you are at, put John Krueger's name on the call list."

What happened next was the congregation called two other pastors. Sometimes it takes a while to figure out what the Holy Spirit wants to do. Sometimes it's a good thing to have a vacancy go just a little longer. Sometimes it is not. This time it was.

When I went to check things out, I discovered that I knew the head elder and his wife. They were from the same small congregation in Wisconsin where I lived from 4th to 7th grade. I didn't know this when we spoke on the phone, but I think he figured out it was I. While I was visiting the calling congregation, the story of how their third call got to me was told.

Will, a respected man in the church, had read all the candidate profiles. He was an attorney, and that's the kind of guy he was. At the call meeting my name was mentioned. Someone pointed out that my profile said I was somewhat impatient. Will stated that perhaps that's what they needed—someone who would endeavor to move things along.

The congregation voted to call me. Subsequently I was at fall pastors' conference in the district I was leaving. I ran into the district president and teased him about putting "somewhat impatient" in my profile. He quipped, "John, I didn't write that," (actually I'm still quite sure he did). "If I had written that, I would have said 'very impatient!'"

But back to Will. Will is one of the smartest people I've had the privilege of having in a congregation. He was an attorney—maybe the first one I ever had—but I was still young! He was a graduate of an Ivy League school—again maybe the only one I ever had. Maybe ever!

Will, however, was very down to earth—a great guy! Two of my remembrances of the way he talked are first of all, his vocabulary. Will not only used words I never used, but some of them I didn't know the meaning of, and one or two of them I had never even heard of! At the same time, Will would use clichés. He'd be talking in his regular educated language, and all of a sudden say things like, "Well her elevator doesn't go all the way to the top!" This often surprised me.

Will was raised in the Lutheran Church—worshiped, I'm sure, every Sunday. Will, like other people my age, knew *The Lutheran Hymnal* very well—never used it for the liturgy, only the hymns. He also knew virtually all the hymn numbers. When we got "the new hymnal," *Lutheran Worship*, he remarked "Well, Pastor John—the new hymnbook is O.K., but now, when I come into church and look at the hymn numbers on the board, I no longer know which hymns we'll be singing." Me either.

One time we were painting the trim on the outside of the

fellowship hall. My other churches called this room Luther Hall, but here it was named Albers Hall after the architect of our original buildings. As I recall, we had already repainted the 30 foot high tilted up concrete sanctuary from top to bottom—colors selected by a wonderful woman who happened to be the treasurer's wife. I'm glad he O.K.'d the funds (see chapter on challenging people!). She had a real flair for decorating and was a joy to work with. I think we recovered the pews to match. This was the church where there was lots of physical repair necessary to go with the congregational health repair. We had already sprayed the acoustical ceiling with 75 gallons of paint, and it was white again.

Now we were on the outside of the building. Will and I were painting side by side, each on his own ladder. It gave him and me a welcomed chance to talk with one another in an unhurried fashion. I don't remember the context, but I do remember Will's words that Saturday morning. I have thought of them many times over the years.

He said, "It really doesn't matter exactly how something is done, but if people of good will are involved, it will be fine." Especially if they are doing it for the Lord.

I think this was part of the inspiration for words I used later on when I had a questionnaire to fill out two churches later, when I was on a call list. I wrote, "At this point in my ministry I have observed that there is always more than one way to do things, and I encourage those who have a plan to carry it out as long as it complements the whole." The result of the work of people of good will.

I was in my office—Will came in. I'm sure he had made an appointment; he simply said he'd like to chat.

Will, of course, was smart. He began by telling me all the good things that were happening at the church and pointed out where he thought I was doing a good job. But then he got to the point. "Pastor John, I am fearful that you are leading us down a dangerous path and the result is going to be a major disappointment for the congregation. I don't believe we are going to raise $100,000 in cash, and many will be disappointed after their expectations that we were going to build initial space for an elementary school are unfulfilled."

This was somewhat early in my ministry and I didn't yet know all the things I know now. In fact, for whatever reason, I was not yet familiar with 3-year capital funding ventures. What I did know at that time was that we could not have an elementary school without classrooms.

We had a great preschool building, but Kindergarten was in half of the fellowship hall, first grade in the other half, and second grade in the church nursery. Third grade would soon be there as we were adding one grade per year, and space was urgently needed.

This isn't the time to talk about congregational meetings, but suffice it to say that the congregation wasn't as excited about building as I was. Actually that was quite often the case! So . . . they said we could build, but only after we had raised $100,000 up front in cash. So . . . I made a big poster with our $100,000 goal.

I did my best to not belittle Will's concern because he was very sincere. What I do remember saying was something like I was relieved his concern wasn't about something more serious (saying this as responsibly as I could, being the blunt and all too often sarcastic person I am). I assured him that I had no doubt that we would reach our $100,000 goal.

We had that goal because the congregation, after having been through some tough (tumultuous?) times, did not just want to borrow and build. I was comfortable with that. I don't remember exactly at what point we were when Will stopped by, but I do remember the day I put a goal poster in the narthex. And I remember one of our ladies saying, "Are we ready for that?" I said, "Yes!"

I don't remember what amount I was able to share with Will

that day, but eventually we had a gift of $28,000, two or three for $5,000, and a host of other donations. And one day, as I was in the preschool playground, for whatever reason, another guy from our church found me, gave a cheery greeting and handed me an envelope. "Here, this is for that project of yours." Returning to my office I opened the envelope to find a check for $10,000. I grabbed my blue magic marker and updated the chart. God is good!

One final note on this donation goal. There was another man, a widower, I think, who was always disgusted that we were raising money for projects, like renovating the restrooms. He said we should not keep bothering the congregation. I thought he had some financial resources and asked him to help with the $100,000. He said that he would see. If, indeed, we were reaching this goal, he would give the last $5,000. When we reached $90,000, he brought me a check.

The building? School offices, library, and classrooms for K, 1, and 2. Then? See the next person of note for the next four classrooms. God is good!

Ella

I met her the first Sunday at our new church. She was very friendly. She was putting her offering in the plate at the entrance to the church. They were not passing the plate for the offering when I first came—that was changed—too many new people thought there was no offering. Some were quite hopeful!

Ella became one of the people with whom I worked closely. She came on evangelism calls with our team. Evangelism was very important to her. The only time she ever chastised me was once when she thought I wasn't taking outreach seriously enough. Oh, and then the time I misspelled her name. "Finally, you put my name in print and then misspell it!"

Actually, Ella didn't expect to be credited for what she did, as you'll soon see. One time, though, she did—don't know why, but she and her husband, a non-member, but still in church every Sunday, decided that there were some windows in the chancel that, even though they were not seen directly, should be stained glass. They let us thank them publically. Like I say, unusual.

Ella's other concern was making sure people had what they needed to do their work—copy machine, type writer (olden days), computer, a decent salary—Ella checked on all these things. If something was missing, it would likely show up at no expense to the church.

One day Ella came in and said my study really needed some work. We ended up with new carpet, new wall coverings, and new furniture. Thanks Ella!

Ella had a personal sense of right and wrong. This extended to the idea that people who did good things should have good things happen to them and vice versa. She loved the book of Esther in the Bible, because those who did evil lost out and those who did good were rewarded. Along this line I remember her telling me one day that one of her sons was going into military service. She said, "I told him that I hoped it would not happen, but if he ever had to shoot an enemy, 'make sure you aim straight'"—her sense of justice.

As I said, I didn't know a lot about capital funding programs at the time, but I did know enough to order building fund envelopes for the next year's offering packs. And I did know that if we got some larger gifts at the beginning, others would be encouraged to give.

I made an appointment with Ella and Bill. He had a responsible position—VP of Finance, I think, with a known business. I prayed about the visit and did the best I knew how, probably a bit amateurish. I showed them the plans. They both looked with interest, although I'm sure Ella had seen them before. I wasn't sure how I was going to transition to asking for a gift, but before I had a chance, Bill took over the conversation.

"So you're here to find out what the Vogelsteins are going to do." With that he pulled something out of his shirt pocket and said, "This is 1,000 shares of stock. What you need to know is that it will go up and it will go down. Yesterday it closed at 28." And I think he said that it was his philosophy that non-profit organizations not play the stock market and probably it should be sold.

On the way out I said, "And Bill, the new adult instruction class begins tomorrow." He said, "I won't be there!" After I took a call to another congregation, happily Bill was baptized by the next pastor.

I knew virtually nothing about the stock market. I remember leaving and thinking, well, it's a thousand shares—closed at 28. So . . . Maybe we have $2,800, or maybe $28,000—I was thinking maybe they would give us $5,000, so you can imagine my astonishment when I discovered it was $28,000.

The next few days as I was still pondering this, the treasurer of the church called me. He said the stock had suddenly risen to $34 a share. He thought we should get it sold. Sounded good to me. I asked how we do that, and we sold it for $35,000 that afternoon.

The next day Ella called me—"Have you sold the stock?" I told her we had. She very quietly said that after it was sold, it went off the market because the company had been sold. The next day it opened at $43/share. I was mortified, realizing that the decision to sell the day before just lost the church $8,000! This mortification lasted quite a while!

The next time I saw Ella, I fell all over myself apologizing. She said two things. First of all, no one, not even her husband the chief financial officer, knew this was going to happen. And second, something that was some of the most gracious and insightful words I would ever hear. "Do not be concerned about this, God wanted our gift to be such and such and that's what it was." Thank you Ella!

A couple of more things I have to say. They are about how Ella could so quickly and succinctly say just the right thing. First, though, I think you'd like to know what Ella, a girl raised in the Midwest, was doing in California.

Ella went to college in Illinois. As she perused the parking lot one day, she noticed a car with a California license plate. In her words, "I said to myself, 'There's my ticket to California!'" Sure enough, resourceful, not to be held back, Ella, she "accidentally" happened by the car just as Bill was returning to it. They were still living happily ever after when I knew them. This "just happened" meeting resulted in four children, and included the wonderful years I was their pastor.

The $100,000 was raised, the first school building was built, we had modest school offices, Kindergarten, first grade, second grade, and a three/four combination, meeting in what was planned to be the library. Fourth grade was added because the principal we called had a fourth grader. This was akin to our adding a grade a year, because the answer to those questioning the future grades of the school were told, "The pastor's son needs another grade next year."

Ella came into my office and said, "We're out of space again, where are we going to put the next grade?" I said, "Would you give that much again?" Ella said, "Maybe more!"

So we had a voters' meeting. The voters were still skeptical, but they voted to build four more classrooms. "But first we have to raise $80,000 up front."

After the vote I was pleased to announce that an anonymous family in the church (Bill and Ella) had issued a challenge that if the congregation gave $40,000, they would match it, and the $80,000 would be in place. They did, and they did, and the new principal made sure the classrooms were built. For the first time we had enough classrooms for our school—the fastest growing Lutheran school in California at that time.

After the announcement of the matching funds, the young woman sitting next to Ella, whispered, "Ella, is that you?" Without a pause, Ella answered, "Where would *we* get that kind of money?" I loved Ella!

In the meantime, my mother went to be with the Lord and Nancy and I were privileged to donate the cabinets in the 6th grade classroom. I figured all our children would then be in that room, but only one was.

The final classrooms for 7th and 8th grades just sort of went up by themselves with an adjustment to the mortgage. Things were going well at the church and school. Another challenging call came, and we moved.

Some years later we learned that Ella went to be with the Lord, joining once more her husband with the California plates. About a year later it was announced that she had left over a million dollars towards the next building project—a Family Life Center. Now basketball can be played indoors and the whole congregation can fellowship at once!

Dave Anderson

Dave Anderson (real name) is a good friend of mine. In fact he made a major impact on my life. Dave was the only one in my church that called me John. By everyone else I was called Pastor John, or if they didn't like me very well, Pastor Krueger.

Dave and Barb Anderson are gospel singers, and have probably been in more Lutheran churches than any other two people in the

United States. I'm confident this is not an exaggeration. They are extremely gracious hosts and we have been invited into their home many times. It was purposely built (with a lot of work by themselves) with Christian ministry in mind. The great room is huge, with several seating areas, and plenty of room for groups to gather, and even mini-concerts to be enjoyed.

My first experience with Dave was in San Francisco, before he was married to Barb. This was in 1970 during the Jesus Movement. I remember the number one song on the radio was "Amazing Grace," by Judy Collins. Calvary Chapel in Southern California was baptizing hundreds of people in the Pacific Ocean. The Charismatic Movement was beginning in full swing with books by Dennis Bennett and Pat Boone. I lived in a Christian commune and we sang from spiral bound *Jesus Style Songs*.

I was on vicarage (seminary internship) in Portland, Oregon and became acquainted with John Rodema, NW Director of Lutheran Youth Alive (LYA). When my pastor introduced me as the new vicar, John said, "Praise the Lord!" I had never heard a Lutheran say that before and was quite perplexed.

LYA was the west coast expression of Lutheran Youth Encounter (LYE). LYE was founded in Minnesota by Dave Anderson as a Lutheran expression of the Jesus Movement. LYE and LYA sponsored youth gatherings with a distinct "We love Jesus, yes we do" spirit. Great fun for Lutheran young people. I was 26 and I, too, loved it.

LYA announced a west coast youth gathering for Thanksgiving weekend of 1970. I loaded kids from my youth group in my car, and we took off down I-5 for a great experience. On stage was this young singer-guy from Minnesota named Dave Anderson. I thought he was pretty cool, and certainly was not afraid to be in front of a crowd.

Throughout the years I ran across Dave and Barb in several places, including at least one church I was pastoring. Once they stayed overnight with us—Dave loved the Blue Diamond almonds produced in Modesto.

When I received the call to Gethsemane, Tempe, I thought of Dave, since it seemed to me that was where Fellowship Ministries, his ministry, was located. I thought maybe he had put me on the call list. He hadn't. It wasn't his church. But the first Sunday I was there, Dave came to check out the new pastor.

I remember the service. I remember saying, "The church exists for those who aren't yet here." A man shouted "Amen" from the choir loft—he turned out to be a really good guy! Dave, also, thought this was good and went home to get Barb for the 2nd service. Sometime later they joined our church. I was always impressed, because even though they were famous in Lutheran circles, at our church they simply competently took part in a very quiet (well not Dave!) way.

The pastors of our circuit (about 12 or so) had an unusual way of meeting together. While most circuits rotated meetings at the circuit churches, our east of Phoenix circuit met for lunch at a hotel in Scottsdale. Most pastors new to the circuit were surprised as I was, but it really was quite nice.

Dave has the spiritual gift of evangelism. One time when he was attending our circuit meeting some of us arrived early. Standing in the lobby, Dave spotted some businessmen seated in the waiting area. He went over to talk to them about the Lord. One of the pastors who knew him well said, "He just can't help himself!" Quite an affirmation of who Dave is.

One of my favorite memories happened when I was at the piano and Dave was standing next to me. I don't remember what song it was, and I'm not sure why Dave was surprised (I think something about the predictable and dull Lutheran thing), but what he said was, "Where did *you* learn to play Gospel?" I wasn't surprised that I played Christian songs with freedom, embellishment, and a bit of lilt; after all I was part of the Jesus movement. And I really enjoy playing the piano!

It was Christmas Eve, I don't remember which year. I think I was at Gethsemane about 4 or 5 years. Dave came into the sacristy after the 5 o'clock service and said, "John that was terrible—no one even knew if you wrote that sermon or read what someone else had written." I have to confirm, that I did a whole lot more reading of sermons than I would have liked to have done. The reason for that was that the words I wrote were the words I wanted to say, and the nuances with which I wrote I thought should be stated exactly that way. On Christmas Eve I'm sure that this was more true than ever.

But Dave didn't stop there. The next thing he said changed my preaching forever. "John, you know what you want to say, you don't have to read it!" I took this as a major compliment, that Dave thought I knew what I wanted to say! Thinking it over, I decided that indeed I did know what I wanted to say, even if I hadn't previously thought of it in those exact words.

At the 7 and 11 o'clock services that evening I left my manuscript behind, got out from behind the pulpit, and, with the exception of funerals, haven't been in one since.

Thank you Lord. Thank you Dave Anderson.

Chapter Two

People of Challenge

T hey are known as alligators—at least that what people at pastors' conference call them. Actually, I think even authors of books on the church call them that. And I know that I've heard more than one speaker call them that. They are challenging people in the congregation.

Think about it. The local congregation is an expression of the Body of Christ in a given location. It has the same assignment as every other part of the Church. Jesus gave two assignments: Love God and people, and make disciples. That's all! In addition, the Holy Spirit gives spiritual gifts (see chapter 13) so that it can happen. 1 Peter 4:10 says, "Each one should use whatever gift he has received to serve others, faithfully administering God's grace in its various forms." So . . . what's the problem?

Easily explained with Luther's words, *simul justus et peccator*— we are at the same time saint and sinner. I would expect that the majority of the challenging people are indeed saints, but the sinner part surely is evident. And in all cases, it might not be their sinful nature at all, but just an over-zealous spirit of wanting to help. But truthfully, I think it's more an over-zealous spirit of wanting things their way. Some of the reasons?

- They were the first ones in the congregation—I always

winced when the words "charter member" were spoken
- They are just obstinate people who don't want things to change
- Over the years everyone has simply let them call the shots
- They are egotistical people
- Their value in life is being important in the church
- They don't understand the concept of humble service
- They have the gift of leadership, but haven't learned "... to serve others, faithfully administering God's grace in its various forms."

Over the years one of the things I learned was that if the congregation were going to function in the best possible way, all those with the spiritual gift of leadership and wanting to use the gift of leadership, needed to work together. And all of them together needed to work with the pastor.

Mitch

Mitch was not a difficult person in the church, rather he was a link between what went on in the parking lot and what went on in church meetings—a wonderful guy! In fact while I'm talking about him, I want to tell you that as an electrician one day he announced he was going to Africa as an electrical missionary. If I remember correctly, he aligned with a Lutheran mission station in western Africa and did their much-needed electrical work. His wife, Sandra, went through my adult instruction class, but before she joined the church insisted on reading the entire Book of Concord—the Lutheran Confessions. Then she joined. Only person I ever had do that, but she wanted to know what she was joining!

Oh, the parking lot? That's where lots of people, difficult and not so difficult, do a lot of talking after meetings. Some actually believe it's the real meeting. Mitch brought those issues to the official meeting where they could actually be acted upon.

Now where were we? Oh yes, challenging people. Let me give a disclaimer first. While I have mixed feelings writing about these people, nevertheless if the writing of this book is about what I observed and learned in the pastoral ministry, this is a real part.

Don

Don was an accomplished person. He had grown children from a previous marriage and was now married to a wonderful person. They had no children. Don would be elected to various offices in the congregation, but I think he liked being president the best. As with many church leaders, Don had lots of ideas. The problem was that he liked to be the person with the information. I remember one time he "discovered a bank account that no one knew was there." Well . . . people knew, but the problem was that the person "in charge" for quite a few years before the current leadership came along didn't share a lot of information or give a lot of reports.

Don was not open to other people's ideas. At this point I have to say something about my personality. It has improved much as I have "observed and learned" over the years, but several times I charged ahead without doing the proper groundwork. This was a long time ago. I think!

So . . . whatever the issue was, Don and I didn't agree on it. Sensing that the congregation was more inclined to go along with what I was thinking, I made a motion at a congregational meeting that was in direct opposition to what Don wanted. It was seconded and passed.

Don was visibly agitated, and if I remember correctly, resigned his position at the end of the meeting.

In looking back, it occurs to me that I was the challenging person! Nevertheless, Don's personality was such that he loved managing crises, whether real or imagined. I often thought that if there weren't a crisis at hand, he would invent one. The outcome? Don took a calmer role in the church, and later on, I took a call. The last time I saw my antagonist, or he saw his(!), he said, "How are you doing?" and gave me a big hug! Sometimes the saint part overrules the sinner part— actually always a good idea!

Ben

Next challenging person—Ben. Ben was identified as someone who should "step back" before I ever came to the church. Stepping back, however, was not one of Ben's characteristics. After I was at the church for a while, Ben offered to do some work. Part of what he did involved making an after-service announcement to the congregation. It was a good announcement and had my blessing.

A few days later, one of the long time members of the church expressed her concern to me. She didn't call Ben by name, but simply said that she was concerned that "the same people [who had caused so many problems in times past, at least in her estimation], the same people were up in front again." Oh my.

Most people are very careful in what they say to the pastor and how they say it—not Ben. Three times Ben told me off in no uncertain terms. And, I would have to say, almost all the difficulty I experienced with Ben had to do with his not being included in decision making as he thought he should be. Actually, this is often the case with difficult people. Wise is the pastor who understands this and is able to figure out how, with integrity, to include them. I wasn't often that wise

Before I mention the three times, I want to tell of the time Ben truly and sincerely made an effort to help me work with him and, at least in his mind, others in the congregation. Ben took me out to lunch and said that when a person (in this case pastor) is leading, he needs to look back once in a while and see if anyone is following. At the time, I thought, "Yes, good advice, but no problem here." What I figured out later was that he wasn't following, and as just said, wanted to be one who was leading.

The first conflict I remember was at the Seder dinner on Maundy Thursday—a great tradition at this church and done every year. One of the things I've learned is hey just leave lots of things alone even if they're not what I think is important.

I knew a great song—perfect Seder dinner song about horse and rider thrown into the sea. I had it all printed up and already on the table. Someone in the kitchen suggested I check with Ben. I called him. He said that, no, they didn't sing at the Seder and if I were going to have a song, I should just count him out of the whole thing.

Next incident was after pro-life Sunday service. He just asked what I was thinking bringing this subject into the church. Well . . .

Third time was Good Friday evening a few years later. As I arrived early to get ready for the service at 7:30, Ben came in with his grandson. He asked where everyone was. I told him the service was at 7:30 and no one else was there yet. Ben was furious. Really. He said the Good Friday service was always at 7 and I should have known that. Then he further lambasted me for not having the service at the time he brought his grandson. You see what I mean about challenging people?

In the meantime you need to know that Ben did lots of good things at the church and earned the right to be involved again. And actually, we were fairly decent friends. However, one time when we were having a kick-off banquet for a 3-year capital funding effort, he had not been included in the leadership team. What was done didn't meet with his approval. I just remember from a distance seeing him come into the banquet room, take a look around, and then storm off. Sometimes being a saint is challenging.

Recently, when visiting this congregation, Ben was one of the greeters in the narthex and warmly voiced his pleasure at seeing us at worship! God is good.

James

James was an educated person. He was respected in the congregation. Over the years he looked after certain things—mostly watching that the congregation did things the way they were supposed to be done. When there was a question of procedure or constitutional correctness at a congregational meeting, no one would talk. Then the chairman would look at James and say, "James?" Then the correct information would be given.

James liked to have things his way. If they were going another direction, he would do what he could to make sure they got turned around. I remember one time when there was a difference of opinion. People on the appropriate ministry team had a meeting and made a decision. One of the people was a person whom James was used to directing—not forcefully, but simply by way of personality. When the result of the meeting was communicated to James, he said no that just wasn't what it should be.

Then he asked about the other person—what he thought. When James understood that the person who usually did his bidding agreed with the rest of us, he simply said, "We'll see about that!"

How did James become the congregational expert? Well . . . he was smart and he was willing. And over the years he and his wife had become very involved. They were good people, and worked hard for the church and school. And there was another dynamic.

The pastor of many years had the spiritual gift of pastor. He did not have the spiritual gift of leadership, and probably not administration. Others needed to fill in, and James simply became the unofficial leader, even though I think the only actual position he held was the ongoing chair of the constitution committee.

James also had a propensity to favor some staff persons over others. I'll just let that statement stand as is.

James made my first 18 months in this congregation much less enjoyable than they would otherwise have been. I had been told that what the church needed was a "strong pastor." I took that to mean a pastor who would get seriously involved in leadership. This seriously compromised James' chief role in the congregation. After 18 months, it became obvious, I believe, to James that he was not able to do things in the church as he had done. He and his wife graciously transferred to another congregation to "go to church with their daughter and grandchild." He left with the appreciation of the congregation for years of service.

Rod

Rod was a person I really liked. In fact, we got along very well and were in the church together for my entire tenure. His wife was very involved and someone I could always depend on. His son was a great teen and his daughter babysat for us. Great family.

So why is Rod in this chapter on challenging people? Actually, I don't think he was as much a challenge for me as I was for him.

Rod was the treasurer. Church treasurers—another story. These dear people take things personally, and they really don't need to. They are all very financially conservative—Rod was at the top of the list.

I was a pastor who always (really—almost always) put the best construction on everything that was said and especially that which was printed. Rod felt it was his responsibility to look at church finances from the most scary point of view. And that's how he wrote his newsletter articles. He actually was fond of the word "bankrupt," as in "We need to be careful not to bankrupt the church."

At my farewell dinner, Rod was one who spoke. It was very funny—I hope he meant it that way!

Rod reiterated, several examples *verbatim*, how what he wrote for the newsletter was edited. He rightly assumed that it was I who made the changes. He willingly volunteered the information that he would write a very cautious summary of the current financial state of the church, only to discover that the way it was finalized in the newsletter sounded rosy, like everything was just peachy keen. Rod and I had many discussions about this. I loved that guy!

Chapter Three

More People

Maynard

Maynard (real name) was a Baptist pastor. I got to know him when I joined in weekly prayer with some of the pastors in the community. It was still during my growing time for understanding the Body of Christ. One morning, Maynard opened his Bible because he wanted to share something. I said to myself, "Why is this Baptist guy using our Bible?" Dumb, I know. But it was an enlightening experience.

I learned that I could trust Maynard, and I was going through a struggle working with someone. I began to think (erroneously, of course, but I was young) that the other staff member got more recognition than I and that he had a better position than I. I became envious, and Maynard was willing to talk to me about this. His counsel was that I should pray that God would bless the person. I replied, "God has already blessed him—that's why I'm envious!"

Maynard said, "Nevertheless, that's what you need to do." So I did, and actually it solved the problem for me. And . . . I learned one of the key principles of Christian living that day—thank God in all situations. "Do not be anxious about anything, but in everything, by prayer and petition, with thanksgiving, present your requests to God." (Philippians 4:6) Over the years, giving thanks to God for whatever was troubling me always worked. My attitude would change, and my faith would grow.

Red

Early in my ministry I lived in a small community. There was a pastors' prayer group, so I joined in. One of the guys was the pastor at the community church. He was an interesting fellow, knowing how to be known. I saw him in town several times before I met him. One time at Friday night football, he was standing, watching the game from the floor in front of the first row of the bleachers. I said to myself, "There's that guy again," and I asked someone who he was. Turned out to be the pastor of the community church; good idea to be seen at town activities!

I have two memories of Red (real name). The first is his telling me that I was born again (I knew that!). He said he could tell by the way I talked and the things I said. He seemed surprised— Evangelicals don't always understand that Lutherans are evangelical too.

The second memory is his telling of the night of his conversion. He had been thinking about spiritual things for a while (God does that, you know). One night he said to himself, "It's no use, she is never going to stop praying for me." All of us who were listening, at least me for sure, thought he was talking about his mother. When asked, he said, "Oh, it was my childhood Sunday School teacher."

"Then Jesus told his disciples a parable to show them that they should always pray and not give up." (Luke 18:1) I'm reminded of two men whose wives prayed for them for years. Interestingly, neither of them was baptized when I was the pastor, but both were a few years after I took a call elsewhere.

Dan

Dan's wife and children joined our church. It was the year we were blessed with nine Baptisms on Easter Eve. Dan was there that evening and his children were baptized, but I don't remember him being at worship any other time. I knew him, because one of his daughters was a regular baby-sitter of our very small children. A few years later, he was baptized and joined the Christian fellowship of the church. ". . . always pray and not give up!"

Bill

At another church, Bill was there every Sunday—actually he was Ella's husband (chapter one). Bill was raised in an unorthodox, quasi Christian denomination. He declined my overtures for instruction, Baptism and church membership. Always at worship, but never at communion. I was gone about three years when all of a sudden, I discovered Bill had been baptized. "She'll never stop praying for me."

Bob

Bob was a great guy. I think he might have been divorced, but sometimes that happens. Bob was a man of faith. I had a Wednesday morning Bible Study for many years. We started with Genesis, and over eight or so years, went through the whole Bible—arriving at one of Paul's letters when I took a call to another congregation. Most of the participants were women, but one of the faithful men was Bob.

Bob had been a professional baseball player. He loved to tell people that he had played ball with Willie Mays. However, his baseball career was cut short. Bob was diagnosed with polio.

Like so many others, Bob had some lasting effects of the disease. He walked stooped over, but when he was sitting his stoop was not noticeable. What happened, however, was that the breathing part of polio returned in his later years. The result was that Bob was in the hospital, on a breathing tube. It was not certain what the result was going to be.

I visited Bob. Because of the breathing tube he, of course, couldn't talk. But that didn't interfere with his thinking. In his ever optimistic way, he got a pencil and paper and wrote a verse he had, as a good Lutheran catechumen, memorized years before. He wrote, "To live is Christ, to die is gain." (Philippians 1:20) Bob was letting me know that he was in the Lord's hands and whatever was ahead was just fine with him.

Bob was moved to nursing care, because without the breathing tube he couldn't live, and with that apparatus he couldn't be at home. I visited Bob again, and a few days later his daughter called to let me know Bob was home with the Lord. She said, "Dad made his decision. He didn't want to live life artificially kept alive any longer. He told the doctor—'I just want to watch the ball game this afternoon, and then please take the tube out.'" As promised, "To die is gain."

Chapter Four

Heartbreaking Experiences

Dora

It was my day off. I was at home. The phone rang. It was the local police department. There had just been a suicide. They wanted a Lutheran pastor. I didn't know the family. I was still quite young; I remember hanging up the phone and saying to myself, "Well— this is about as tough as it gets. After this anything else ought to be easier."

I arrived at the home. Dora was sitting in the living room. There were a couple of police officers in the house. Dora was crying. I sat next to her and asked what had happened. "My husband shot and killed himself. His body is still in the bathroom."

One of the officers said, "No one should really go in there until the bathroom has been attended to." The whole thing was very gory.

There are things that happen to some families that are above and beyond what an average person, including me, thinks should ever happen. This day's happening was only part of the abysmal series of events this family went through.

Dora turned out to be a very fine lady. She and her husband had been away from church for some time—that happens all too often when there is a move to a new community, and the church in which people were active is not replaced in the move. Dora found a new

35

church home with us and with people who cared about her. I did the service for her husband.

Dora had two grown daughters. One of them wasn't close, but the other one, Jan, joined our church and had her child in our preschool. The suicide was just the beginning of our ministry to Dora and her family.

I don't clearly remember the details, but Jan's former husband's car was discovered in a remote area a ways out of town. His body was in the car—he had taken his life. I was astonished that Jan had now experienced suicide for the second time. First, her step father, and now her ex-husband. I didn't have the service, I'm not even sure there was one, but we continued to care for Jan and Dora.

It wasn't long after that Dora was diagnosed with cancer. Again, I wondered, "why," and "what more could happen to this dear lady?" I visited her in the hospital. She was in good spirits. We prayed. She said she was in the hands of the Lord whatever lay ahead. Statements like that always are meaningful to me.

The next time I visited Dora in the hospital, she wouldn't talk to me. Regardless of my approach, there was a determined silence. Her entire face showed anger, maybe even contempt. This simply was not the Dora who previously was appreciative and responsive to all my pastoral care. I, of course, prayed, even though there was no indication that I had permission to do that. I left the hospital in a state of confusion. It took some time for me to come to an understanding of what happened that day.

A few days later, with some apprehension, I went to visit again. Not knowing what to expect, I entered the room to a cheery voice saying, "Hi Pastor John!" All was back to normal, as normal as it can be when someone is dying of cancer. We talked and prayed.

When Dora went home to be with the Lord, I had her service, giving peace to her daughters. It is a joy to minister with the love of the Savior, through Whom we have total confidence of what follows this life.

In thinking about that one uncomfortable day, I came to the conclusion that the four stages of loss are very real: denial, anger, bargaining, and acceptance. Dora went through them all. The behavior expressed during her stage of anger, showed how very real this was. In the end, the Lord led her to peaceful acceptance, anticipating the joy of heaven.

Joel

I was at district pastors' conference. I called home to see how things were going. Nancy told me that Mary had called and was on her way out of state. Her son, Joel, had gone to see his father and had been shot. That's all Nancy knew.

When I got home the next day, the first thing Nancy said was, "Joel's dead." I couldn't believe it. Joel had died instantly, but when they called Mary, they were very kind not to tell her the outcome, sparing her the agony of a plane flight knowing her son was dead.

Mary and her children were active members of our church. I had confirmed Joel and there was no doubt he was in heaven, but lived only to be a teenager. The story is so tragic that I wasn't going to include it without asking Mary's permission. During the writing of this book, we visited the church where Mary and her family had been members. I couldn't believe it when Mary ended up sitting next to me for worship. I took the opportunity to tell her what I was doing. She expressed positive feelings about this.

Joel's death was not only tragic, it was bizarre. Joel and his friend were target shooting out by the barn. After shooting, they went into the barn and started cleaning the gun. Joel's dad came into the barn and told the boys to go do some chores. While they were out, he finished cleaning the gun, and unbeknownst to the boys, reloaded the gun and placed it on the shelf. When the boys later returned, still assuming the gun was unloaded (Joel's friend had the bullets in his pocket), Joel's friend picked up the gun and pretended to shoot Joel.

Joel fell to the floor. His friend said, "Come on, Joel. Get up. Get up!" Joel didn't get up.

The memorial service was in our church. It was tough. I'm sort of an unrealistic person, and had decided that although I would be a pastor, I didn't ever want to do the service for a child. This was the first of several.

What I remember most was coming into the fellowship hall after the service and finding teenage boys crying. These were guys that never showed this kind of emotion.

The only person at a Christian's funeral who is not saddened, is the person who died. Joel was with the Lord—enjoying a completed relationship. The rest of us were sad, but comforted (maturation of this comfort would take a while) knowing that God is able to take care of us in all situations.

Mary continued to be an active member of our congregation, her life blessed as God continued to be with her and Joel's sister.

Rick

I was on my way to bed when the phone rang. It was Rick's dad. "There's been an accident. Rick had a serious fall. Can you come to the hospital."

I met Rick's mom and dad in the hospital lobby. I asked where he was and they said he was in ICU—intensive care unit. I said that it was this way and started down the hall. Rick's mom said it was nice being with someone who knew where they were going. Pastors do know their way around the hospitals in the community.

Rick was lying in bed—I don't remember if he was on a ventilator—I don't think so, but he did have an oxygen mask over his nose and mouth. In the next few minutes I learned that he had broken his neck and was severely injured. How severely? I asked if Rick, an avid soccer player, would be able to play on Saturday. "No." By Christmas? "We'll see."

One of the nurses told Rick's mom and dad, all too soon, that they needed to just forget Rick the way he was yesterday, and see what they could do to help Rick as he is now. Rick's mom, understandably, was very upset.

How severely? The next day as I was walking down the hall of the hospital, by chance I ran into one of the medical doctors from our church. I told him what had happened. I said that I sure hoped Rick would walk again. From the look on his face and the words he spoke as kindly as he could, I realized that whatever I hoped, he was sure that wouldn't be the case.

Rick's mom and dad had been at a home Bible study. The kids, including this young teenager, were outside playing. Crawling over a fence, Rick's pant leg got stuck on the top of the fence, and Rick fell headfirst, breaking his neck. At exactly which vertebrae this happens determines the extent of the paralysis.

I watched carefully in my next visits. Rick could talk. Rick could move his fingers. Later he could move his arms. He could not walk. This was a major injury.

I had friends in the community who were pastors. I trusted them and told them this story. Along with the family, I was very upset that this had happened. So, of course, was the entire congregation. They all knew Rick. I questioned the pastors, "I just don't see how God lets something like this happen." The answer I got was, "The devil is on a leash, but sometimes the leash is quite long."

This incident was years ago. Rick comes from a family of believers. Together we know that God is present in all circumstances and that He can use even tragedy for His purposes. No . . . Rick did not play soccer again, but he to this day is a demonstration that life continues, even grows, in the face of tragedy.

Rick had the best care and the best therapy. He persisted. He worked a long time to be the person he is today. He learned to use a computer via a stick in his mouth. He became very proficient in operating his electric wheel chair. A grand day it was when there was whispering in the church and people turned around to watch Rick, leaning on a walker, and slowly coming into the sanctuary on his own.

Rick went back to his own high school, where he was a top student. One year he was homecoming king—showing how much he inspired the kids at his school. Today Rick is a college graduate, and works as a college sports/physical administrator.

Tragedy is never good in life. However regardless of how one's life and one's family's life is changed, God's love, inspiration and energy are there to help heart breaking experiences be overcome.

Baby

Sometimes it's hard to believe the unimaginable dreadfulness of an event. No matter how one looks at it, contemplating the details only makes it worse. The baby of one of our families was with her trusted baby sitter. She was in the playpen in the spare room, taking a nap. Hanging on the closet door next to the playpen, was a bag containing clothes brought back from the dry cleaners.

The bag was flimsy cellophane. The air conditioner came on. The cellophane bag blew in the circulating air from the vent. It blew over the baby's face, and the baby suffocated.

I was called to the hospital. There in the room was the sobbing mother and the horrified father. The baby was lying on a raised bed, with a not-needed ventilator tube in her mouth. Wanting to help, I summoned a hospital attendant and asked that the tube be removed, so the parents could hold their child unimpeded. I was told "No." There are some things I just don't understand. The baby was dead, and in my opinion, this was simply an indignity.

I encouraged them to hold the baby, tube and all.

The service at the mortuary took place, of course, in sadness. Were it not for the Lord, there had been no hope at all. It was a chance, however, for family and friends to show their love. The message of the day focused on the wonder of eternal life that their baby was experiencing in God's presence.

Besides the parents and the people in their lives, another suffering person was the babysitter. She wasn't at the funeral, but she did all she could to express her remorse and reach out to the family in love. God's grace is needed many, many times in this world.

Paul

I had just gotten home from church. There was a phone message—a person from a hospital in a larger city a few miles away. "There's been an accident, would I please call her." I did.

She told me that there had been an accident, and Paul had been killed. Would I please come to the hospital, the family wanted to see me. I went immediately.

When I parked and, walking across the parking lot, approached the hospital, I saw them. The dad, the older sister and younger brother, and a friend I knew quite well. I didn't have to say anything, they were ready to tell me everything. Would I please go with them into the room where Paul was. They had not yet seen him. He had been brought to the hospital by emergency workers.

My immediate thought, of course, was, "This is the part of the ministry that is really difficult." But at the same time, this is a part of the ministry that is so very important, so very much appreciated, and such a poignant opportunity to share the love of Christ.

We went into the room. Paul's body was lying on a raised gurney. I don't have to describe the scene—you can fully imagine the dismay and sorrow in the room. Once again, there was a tube in Paul's mouth. From my non-medical point of view, I just don't see why that has to be. Paul's father looked at him and said, "Foolish, foolish boy." What had happened?

Paul was 14. He and a friend or two (whose lives were also changed forever), were riding their bikes over at the university in the parking garage. They enjoyed riding to the top of the ramps and then coasting (unfortunately wildly) down the ramps to the lower levels. Actually, not coasting, but racing. Paul's friend came to the end of the 4th floor ramp and made it around the corner. Paul did not. His bicycle hit the guard rail and Paul flew over the rail and was killed as he hit the ground below.

Finally, Paul's family left the hospital, as did I. I met with them the next day and we planned the funeral. They sent me home with the talk Paul had written for his Confirmation a few months earlier. The kids had an assignment to write three short essays. "Why I want to be confirmed," "My faith in the Lord Jesus Christ," and "My favorite Bible verse and what it means to me." I would then choose the one I wanted them to read on Confirmation Day. They read them at the point in the service where there would have been the congregation's statement of faith using the creed.

At the time of Paul's Confirmation, I hadn't noticed anything unusual, but now, reading what he had written, it was almost as if he knew he would be with the Lord a lot sooner than anyone would have imagined. It was a real testimony of his confident faith in the Lord Jesus and his unreserved expectation of being in heaven with Him some day.

The funeral was held in the Family Life Center (gym) so that there would be room. The chairs were filled with family and friends including many from the congregation. The bleachers were filled with students from Paul's school.

It was a meaningful service. I read Paul's Confirmation essay. And when it was time for my message, I found myself walking over to the bleachers and telling the kids the Good News of Jesus. It was one of the most meaningful opportunities of my ministry to share the Gospel! My prayer then, and still now, is that they would be blessed by what they heard, and receive the same confidence of eternal life that Paul had and was now already experiencing.

Paul's family, of course, had their lives changed in a most dramatic way. They were regularly at worship, and over the next few months his sister no longer cried when she saw me. The younger brother's countenance changed without his big brother, but he, too, grew in faith and understanding the love of God.

"For I am convinced that neither death nor life, neither angels nor demons, neither the present nor the future, nor any powers, neither height nor depth, nor anything else in all creation, will be able to separate us from the love of God that is in Christ Jesus our Lord." (Romans 8:38-39)

Chapter Five

Special Messages

I'm going to do this roughly in chronological order, as I remember people who have told me they personally have been in God's presence in a special way or who have heard Him speak to them. The stories are amazing, and I have no doubt that they are true.

Emma

Emma was a very down to earth Lutheran woman. She had the spiritual gift of hospitality, and even though she lived in a very modest home, she would invite the friends of her son to stay with her when we visited in Wisconsin. We, as seminary students, were there every so often because there were girlfriends living there!

Emma's husband went to be with the Lord. Sometime later, she told of an experience she had. She was resting in the living room, when she became aware of a bright light in the kitchen. She wondered what it might be. As she got up, she wondered if indeed it were her time to join her dear husband in heaven. Then the impression from the Light clearly was—"I just want you to know that even though your husband died, I am with you, and all will be O.K." I can't tell you enough, how very plain-spoken Emma was. I think that's important!

Ruth

The next person, Ruth, was a bit more ditzy—that is she tended to be a bit outspoken and off the cuff. But . . . she, too, saw God's presence. It was the same light, except it happened while she was sitting at a lunch counter. I don't know anything about others seeing the Light, but I do know that Ruth's life was changed. She had not been walking with the Lord, and her life was characterized by careless living, including a foul mouth (glad I didn't know her before!). Ruth's lifestyle underwent an immediate revision, and when I knew her she was active in the church, graciously serving the Lord and His people.

Marie

Person three—Marie. Again, this person was very down to earth, matter of fact, and not by any means a person of exaggeration. She was a long time member of the congregation, who had stayed during a time of turmoil. I remember the first time I was at the church, noting the seeming neglect. In the pastor's study was a drapery rod that was falling off the wall at one end. I got to appreciate that rod as symbolic of a somewhat sagging congregation.

A short time after taking the call and becoming the pastor of this church which had previously been twice as big as it was now, I was in the fellowship hall with Marie. I don't remember what we were doing there, but I do remember saying, "Let's get these chairs put away." The folding chairs were folded up, standing helter-skelter against the walls. Marie said, "I just love it! No one has cared about anything for so long. I just love it."

Sometime later Marie and I were talking about something. I don't remember what it was, but Marie said "This is important. I know what

45

we are doing is important. Pastor, I know because I've seen God." This statement always is amazing no matter how you look at it.

Marie almost died giving birth to her second child. As this was occurring, there was a bright light in the delivery room. From the Light came the words that it wasn't her time—she would stay and raise her children. And she did.

Clarence

The next person was a man—Clarence. Clarence was a no-nonsense Dutchman. I really didn't know too many Dutchmen, except the dozens of families I grew up with in Friesland, Wisconsin, until I was ten years old. All I knew then, was most of their names had "ma" at the end, and they went to the Reformed Church, rather than to the Lutheran Church. Didn't realize at the time that we were all on the same side! But I digress.

Clarence was a patient in the hospital when he saw the Light. He recognized immediately that it was God's presence, and had the impression that God was there to grant a request. Clarence was recovering nicely, so he simply said (prayed), "Lord, I'm doing just fine, but would you help my buddy?" In the bed next to Clarence was a man suffering to the point that there was constant moaning. When he said "would you help my buddy" the moaning stopped and the man rested comfortably. God is good!

Ralph

Then there are those who've heard God's voice. First my friend

Ralph. Ralph was special no matter how you looked at it. The congregation started in his living room with five families present. Ralph was like the church father. He did things that were out of the ordinary. He was fascinated with parts of Scripture of which others may not even have heard. He once did a Christmas program on "the begats," with a whole host of biblical characters parading down the aisle. I think Mary and Joseph showed up at the end!

One summer Ralph volunteered to be in charge of vacation Bible school. I think he had a plan, but no one else knew what it was. He had no preliminary meetings, and forgot to recruit staff, so on the first morning of VBS, Ralph was out in the parking lot. As mothers came to drop off their children, he simply met them as they walked across the parking lot and told them which class he'd like them to teach. I probably shouldn't have told you that, because what comes next should not be discounted.

Ralph heard the voice of God. I don't remember all the details, but it had something to do with the idea for a cartoon based on the premise of "Try Again and Succeed." Somehow God spoke this idea to him. The cartoon won an academy award.

Al

The next person who heard the voice of God is, in my opinion, the most poignant of these seeing and hearing God accounts. This, again, was a very down to earth gentleman. He was a good friend—faithfully at Saturday morning Men's Bible Study with the guy who saw the Lord in the hospital. Al also was my friend because he owned an almond ranch and gave us a big box of shelled almonds every fall that lasted until the next fall. I miss those to this day!

Al was a platoon leader during WW II. He served in a war zone. One day he was leading his men through the woods. God told him, "Turn right here." The plan was not to turn at that point but to continue straight ahead. Nevertheless, Al turned right and his men followed. Immediately thereafter, there was a major explosion just where they would have been had they continued going straight ahead. Al and his guys were safe.

Betty

The next dear person is a woman who became a good friend of mine. Betty was standing in the narthex one day, and since I didn't know who she was, I went over to talk to her. That was the beginning. She had been away from the church for a long time, but soon was very active—one of those people who could always be counted on.

On New Year's Eve I didn't preach. I told them that I chose the songs and gave the message the rest of the year, so on New Year's Eve, those present shouted out hymn numbers and we sang them. I loved it because I insisted on playing the piano, which I didn't get to do very often. The sermon consisted of those who were willing to get up and give a testimony or tell us for what they were thankful the past year.

Betty usually had something to say. I think it was on one of these occasions that she shared how she got to the church. Betty lived in the neighborhood and would drive by our church property, which was on a major street (good planning). I recently checked with Betty to make sure I got this right.

One day as she was driving by God said to her, "Jesus is there. You need to be there." So she came. When I was checking on this Betty wrote, "Please quote God correctly! And I think you'll need a whole chapter to cover your 'experiences' with me." Sorry, Betty, this is all I'm going to say.

Me

What a joy it is to know people who have had these real life experiences with the Lord. He works in various ways, He works in mysterious ways. My experience is that He dramatically talks to me in what happens in my life.

One time He sent me an angel. I was a very young pastor, maybe the first year of my ministry. I served a very small congregation as a worker-priest. I'm not sure what I was expecting, but it wasn't happening. In the message that morning, I told the congregation that I was discouraged and specifically listed several things. I don't remember what else the message was about, but I do remember what the angel told me at the door.

He appeared as a well-groomed gentleman of about 50 years, wearing a suit. Outside of the surmise that he was an angel, I have no idea of what he was doing in our small town. I shook his hand, and he looked me straight in the eye and said, "Young man, it is not your job to tell people you are discouraged, it is your job to encourage them with the Good News of Jesus Christ." Wow! I learned so very much that morning.

Chapter Six

Bitterness Gone

Not too long ago I was looking at the photo album my mom made for me when I grew up. As I paged through it I was struck by a picture of my dad on the sun porch of my childhood home in Friesland, Wisconsin. He was holding a baby and looking at the camera with a big grin on his face. He looked thrilled, the picture of delight. I contemplated the picture, wondering exactly what was going on, and then realized the baby was I and this was the day of my Baptism.

I sadly said out loud, "Look at this picture. What happened?"

Well I don't know what happened, but following are excerpts of what I experienced beginning in that home in Friesland, a German and Dutch small town of 352 people, in south central Wisconsin. As I think about writing this part of the story, I realize that it begins very negatively—I suppose those memories stand out. However, please know that my dad raised a fine family and was a wonderful pastor!

My dad was born in Menomonee, Wisconsin in 1903. He was the 5th of seven children. His parents were German immigrants. As near as I can figure out, his dad may have been one of the founding fathers of St. Paul's Evangelical Lutheran Church. My grandparents' graves are in St. Paul's cemetery, as are all their children's graves except my parents, whose graves are in North Burnett, Wisconsin across the road from where I went to one-room country school, after leaving Friesland when I was ten.

Dad, (as did my mom, and incidentally, Nancy) went to only Lutheran schools his entire education. He graduated from Wisconsin Lutheran Seminary in Wauwatosa, Wisconsin in 1927. It was ice skating in Washington Park in Milwaukee that he legendarily met my mother. They were married in 1928, while Dad was serving his second call in Hettinger, North Dakota. He later received the call to Friesland (dual parish with Dalton), and in 1954 took a call to North Burnett, and into The Lutheran Church - Missouri Synod. But I digress. I think the problem was mainly that Dad did not understand compliments nor encouragement. He did understand discipline, which was fine, and criticism, which was not. When I was taking a marriage and family course during my doctoral studies, I was reading an assigned book, and came across a chapter entitled, "German Fathers." I read this with amazement, saying over and over again, "This is my dad!"

Two memories sort of sum up my experience. Both of them happened in Spencer, Wisconsin, where we lived during my high school years. (Later, when Dad took a pre-retirement call to Poy Sippi, a town where none of us had ever lived, my dad astutely observed, "We should have moved here sooner. The kids have no friends here, and when they come home they stay home with us." I thought that was cool. But I digress!)

Living in a parsonage, the sidewalk in front of our house shared a lot line with the church property. We kept up the parsonage yard, the janitor did the church's yard. In Wisconsin it snows. Sometimes a lot. I was a good son (no, really, I was), and shoveled the front walk. When I was finished, there never was a thank you. One time I was criticized for going too far, "doing the janitor's work." The next time, I shortened the boundary. "You want the janitor to think we're taking advantage of him?"

One time it was summer. I was home alone. My folks had gone shopping. I, without being asked (I told you I was a good son), cleaned the garage. Thoroughly. Including moving everything and hosing it out. I thought, "This time Daddy will be really happy and give me a compliment."

When he and Mom came home, they had packages in their arms, unloading the car. I said, "Daddy—look at the garage, I cleaned it!" His only response was "Did you do the basement, too?"

And that's how it was.

When I was leaving for Madison, for my junior year of college (the first two were in Wausau, closer to home), I went in to say good bye to my dad. He hugged me and said, "I love you kids so much, I wish you would love me." And so I went away.

Oh—I think I should tell you a couple of good things—when I was in 8th grade, my parents bought a full two manual organ with full foot pedals for our home. Really it was for me. That was good! And . . . when I was 16, they bought a ski boat, and let us kids take it out by ourselves—a lot! That was very good!

So the years went by with me not liking my dad. We, of course, were cordial, maybe even loving, but I got very tired of him telling me (an adult, pastor, father) what to do. So I told him that I really didn't appreciate his advice. After that he said, "Now I know you don't want me to say this . . ." And then he continued telling me what he thought I should do. Once I tried to get our relationship straightened out, but even that didn't go well. Sure wish he were here now that I'm old enough to know a few things!

So the years went by with me not liking my dad . . . until . . .

It was at one of the Church of Modesto's (see chapter 8) prayer summits. The leaders from Multnomah Bible College in Portland, Oregon, instructed us, "This morning the prayers will all begin, "I love you Lord because . . ." Try that sometime—it works well.

There was among us a cool guy, sort of eccentric, from Turlock. He would always pray calling God "Daddy," and telling Him he was climbing up on His lap.

This morning he prayed, "I love you Lord because you gave me my father. Oh, he wasn't a very good father, he was a drunk and he beat me. But he was the best daddy he knew how to be."

Halfway through this the tears were running down my face—I am emotional even as I write this. The tears were running down my face, and I said to myself, "My dad wasn't a drunk, and my dad didn't beat me. And my dad, too, was the best daddy he knew how to be." Instantaneously, the bitterness left, and has not come back! Thank you Jesus! Forgiving someone and leaving bitterness behind is a wonderful thing. It comes from God and is a blessing.

Two additional observations. I now realize that our strained relationship was not all my father's fault—I contributed as well. And . . . I so much would love to have a conversation with Dad about lots of different things. Being in my sixties, I not only understand a whole lot more about lots of things, I also understand some of the things my dad said and did. He was a pastor, too, and knew a lot about that! But I didn't know he knew!

And the final chapter hasn't yet been written. I look forward to seeing him again. That wasn't always true, but it is now!

Part Two

God works in wondrous ways to establish and continue relationships with people. The Bible, inspired Scripture, is the communication of His understanding and work in the world, past and present.

In addition, God has established the mission and ministry of the Church in the local congregation. What follows is an appreciation for what God has done and what He continues to do. This is intermingled with insight as to the workings of a congregation.

Chapter Seven

Meaningful Scripture

We were in the Garden of Gethsemane in Israel. I was privileged to be the tour pastor as Kevin Saunders of *Logos Bible Studies* led a trip to the Holy Land. My wife, Nancy, had studied through the Bible with Kevin over a five year period, as did a number of our Gethsemane members. Kevin invited me to be the accompanying pastor.

Being in Israel was a transformation in my understanding. I believe that all seminary students should be required to go before graduation. Surely there are Christians with the means to endow such a program. When we returned to Arizona, I reported to the congregation that indeed this was a wonderful experience, and I wanted them to know that just outside of Jerusalem there is a garden on the Mount of Olives that is named after our church!

In the Garden of Gethsemane, Kevin asked me to lead a devotion. I immediately knew what I wanted to do, because one of my favorite Bible passages took place there.

When the temple guards came to the garden to arrest Jesus, He asked them, "'Who is it you want?' 'Jesus of Nazareth,' they replied. 'I am he,' Jesus said. When Jesus said 'I am he,' they drew back and fell to the ground." (John 18:4-6)

I love this, of course, because it was an acclamation that Jesus is indeed God. I love it because of the power of that declaration; and I love it because of the acclamation "I AM!"

After I had concluded the devotion, Kevin said that I was going to really enjoy The Church of All Nations, also on the Mount of Olives, which we would be visiting next. Sure enough, when I saw the front of the sanctuary, I was delighted. In a floor to ceiling painting was Jesus with a narrow ring of white drawn around Him. Also there were the soldiers, reeled back to the ground. This was expected. But what really caught my eye, were the trees, blown back, leaning away from Jesus with a "Wow" expression in their demeanor. Even the flames on the soldiers' torches were leaning away from the Son of God.

Another favorite passage is the conversation Jesus had with the Jews about His identity, coming from the Father and sharing His glory. The discussion includes the importance of Abraham. Finally Jesus says, "'I tell you the truth . . . Before Abraham was born, I am!'" (John 8:58) Recognizing exactly what Jesus was saying—that He identified with Yahweh—I AM, they picked up stones to stone Him for blasphemy.

There are stones involved in another favorite passage of mine. When Jesus entered Jerusalem on Palm Sunday, ". . . the whole crowd of disciples began joyfully to praise God in loud voices for all the miracles they had seen: 'Blessed is the king who comes in the name of the Lord!'" (Luke 19:37-38)

Some of the Pharisees reprimanded Jesus for allowing this—they wanted Him to rebuke the people. Jesus simply said that it wouldn't do any good, because if there were not human praise, then the stones on the road would cry out—such was the importance of His identity and His mission for coming into Jerusalem.

Immediately after is another, but actually closely connected. "As he approached Jerusalem and saw the city, he wept over it and said, "If you, even you, had only known on this day what would bring you peace . . ." (Luke 19:41-42) How different the world would have been and very likely would be today, if Jerusalem had accepted Jesus. No wonder He wept.

As I think about these favorite passages of mine, I note that they have something in common—the identity of Jesus the Christ, the Savior of the world. Praise be to God!

Then there are some incidents along the way of Jesus' 3-year ministry of teaching, healing, and application of God's way to live. They involve requests for healing. In John 4 there is a royal officer in Cana whose son was sick at Capernaum. He had heard of Jesus and asked him to come and heal his son, who was close to death. Jesus, wanting to use this as a teaching moment turned the conversation to people's need to see signs and wonders. This was not what the man wanted to talk about—he had a heartfelt need, so he said to Jesus, "Sir, come down before my child dies."

In His compassion, Jesus stopped making His point, and said, "You may go. Your son will live." And of course he was healed at that moment and lived. God is good!

There was another man, with a similar need, but not quite as much daring. This is in Mark 9:14 ff where a father says to Jesus, "But if you can do anything, take pity on us and help us." Jesus was incredulous. "If you can?" Of course He could, and as in Luke 5:12-13, when a man asked Jesus if He were willing (of course He was), Jesus did the healing.

And still another—maybe the one I like the most, because it was a man of faith and position, who understood power and authority. This is the centurion in Capernaum in Matthew 8:5, who asked for healing for his servant, lying at home ". . . paralyzed and in terrible suffering." Jesus said, "I will go and heal him." The man told Jesus to just say the word of healing, since he was not worthy to have Him come to his home. Then he explained the authority he had, and knew the authority that Jesus had. "When Jesus heard this, he was astonished and said to those following him, 'I tell you the truth, I have not found anyone in Israel with such great faith.'" I love that!

One more passage, but a very different subject. It is a double entendre. It was the evening before Jesus was crucified. Lots happened that evening, but for me, one of the verses that sums it all up is John 13:30, "As soon as Judas had taken the bread, he went out. And it was night." During the last supper, the sun went down. But also that evening and the next day, spiritual darkness would play its role. As horrific as that would be, it was not the end—for with the dawn of Sunday, the ultimate Light of God's love for us would be dramatically seen! "He is risen, indeed! Alleluia!"

And a couple more. There are passages in Scripture that truly need some thought, not only spiritually, but simply to make sense. Two come to mind. The first is also from the Passion Narrative. Jesus is before Pilate. Jesus is quiet, and Pilate says, "Do you refuse to speak to me? Don't you realize I have power either to free you or to crucify you?" (John 18:36) Jesus answers, "You would have no power over me if it were not given to you from above. Therefore the one who handed me over to you is guilty of a greater sin." What does this mean?

In my understanding, the greater sin is assuming that Pilate had more authority than God who was orchestrating the sacrifice for the sins of the world. It is a great sin to execute someone who is innocent, but it is a greater sin to not be in obedience to God.

And one more, which took me some time to figure out. This is the account of the dishonest steward who was fired, but while his signature was still legal, discounted the debts owed his master. When I was a kid I couldn't figure out what was going on and how he could do that, but, now, of course, it's as stated. Then . . .

"The master commended the dishonest manager because he had acted shrewdly. For the people of this world are more shrewd in dealing with their own kind than are the people of the light. I tell you use worldly wealth to gain friends for yourselves, so that when it is gone, you will be welcomed into eternal dwellings." (Luke 16:8-9)

First of all, an observation that when it comes to cheating in business, sincere Christians are no match for unbelievers. But then . . . Jesus transitions to another topic. He is telling Christians to use their material resources to bring people to the Lord (e.g. missions, but certainly lots of other ways). Then . . . those going to heaven before the death of the Christian whose wealth provided opportunity for them to hear the gospel, will be in heaven to welcome them when they get there. What a great way to further the Kingdom!

Maybe all these passages are obvious, and maybe I'm just a slow learner, but I think that God's Word is amazingly clever!

Chapter Eight

The Body of Christ

" **A** nd I believe in one holy Christian and apostolic Church."
The question, then, is "How has this belief been experienced in my life?"

Oh my! Well, let's just tell the story. It of course includes my "observation and learning." It includes the way some denominations, including my own, say this, but in my opinion, don't always act in a way that demonstrates this confession. And . . . great is the blessing in my life, how I have experienced one holy Christian and apostolic Church.

I was baptized into the one holy Christian and apostolic Church in a denomination that today (not quite so much as then, but very much nevertheless) sees itself as having the true teaching of the Church, in all that this implies. This denomination not only does not have altar and pulpit fellowship with other Christians, they practice selective prayer fellowship, so there is no worship or prayer with other Christians. That's where I started!

When I was ten, our family transferred (possible then, but not now) to another Lutheran Church body. Throughout my teenage years, and into college, I grew to love The Lutheran Church - Missouri Synod (LCMS, or simply referred to as the Missouri Synod), being extensively involved with North Wisconsin District Walther League (youth group named after the first president of the LCMS.)

Then, attending the University of Wisconsin in Madison beginning my junior year of college, I was active at Calvary Chapel, the LCMS student congregation right next to the university. I remember thinking one day on my way up the stairs into the building, "I truly enjoy being a Christian, and am really blessed not only being a Lutheran, but being part of the LCMS, the best church body in the world." So shoot me, but I remember that incident very clearly.

Now . . . while I continue to love the Missouri Synod—I am on the roster of "ordained ministers" of "The Lutheran Annual,"—at least until this chapter is read (!), my understanding of the Church and especially church unity, fellowship, and with whom we ought to worship, is much broader. So . . . what happened?

I think it started on vicarage (pastoral internship). I was assigned to a historic LCMS church in downtown Portland, Oregon (learned how to properly pronounce Oregon the first day I was there!). This was 1970—the Jesus movement was in full swing, the charismatic movement was getting dynamically off the ground (actually it was never on the ground!), Nicky Cruz was made famous through the writing of *The Cross and the Switchblade* by David Wilkerson, an Assemblies of God evangelist (little did I know at that time that my children would one day graduate from an Assemblies of God high school) and Judy Collins singing "Amazing Grace" was at the top of the popular music charts.

On the west coast, the Lutheran part of the Jesus Movement was Lutheran Youth Alive, a great organization doing ministry largely through regional and local concerts. The NW leader was John Rodema, who left his employment to open his home to foster children and head up LYA. This time period, the west coast, and all the above was really a new experience for me.

When I met John Rodema in the pastor's office and was introduced as the new vicar, he said, "Praise the Lord!" I had never heard a Lutheran say "Praise the Lord" before (except in the traditional liturgy where we sang it three times in Latin following the epistle reading—"Hallelujah! Hallelujah! Hallelujah!"—I don't make these things up!), and wasn't sure what to make of it. A couple years later when my mother met some of my Agape House friends, she didn't know what to make of it either!

Reading *The Cross and the Switchblade*, the story of a small church pastor in Pennsylvania who went to New York City to tell the gangs about Jesus' love for them, quite literally changed my life. (It is one of the few books I still have on my bookshelf, having giving away the major portion of my library when I retired.) They say "If you don't get converted on vicarage, you really can't be a pastor!" Of course "converted" here is not in the sense of "being saved." And so in a few short months my Christian understanding and dedication changed dramatically.

At Zion, Portland, there were five active young adults in their early twenties. This was the time of communes, and to make a long story short, the six of us got together, legally incorporated as "Agape House, Inc." and bought a charming three-story house in close-in SE Portland. It was filled with singing, Bible study, prayer, and ministry to forlorn, misplaced, needy singles. God blessed this so dramatically.

Along came James. James, I'm pretty sure, was a Lutheran, but he was also charismatic. James was one of the most dedicated followers of Christ I had ever met. Interesting. His being a non-traditional Lutheran, led me to observing and learning that the one holy Christian and apostolic Church was indeed broader than my Midwest Lutheran experience.

My first call, following graduation from Concordia Seminary in

St. Louis, was to a tiny church in Burney, CA, where I was a worker priest—needed to make money at secular employment. My father was incensed! "First he had to work his way through college and seminary, and now he has to work his way through the ministry!" I think I was somewhat disappointed myself, but I had prayed (very specifically, on my knees in my dorm room) about where I would be placed, and I trusted God that this was what He wanted. Turns out it was!

In Burney, for whatever reason, I got into a prayer fellowship with other pastors (non-Lutheran!) in town. One of my memories is the pastor of Grace Community Church. He was the person who became a pastor because his childhood Sunday School teacher never stopped praying for him and he finally decided he had better follow Jesus because she wasn't going to give up. True story.

One day this pastor said to me (don't remember the context) that I was born again. Actually, this isn't as strange as it sounds, because in the Body of Christ, it's not only Lutherans who are suspicious of others, the others are suspicious of Lutherans as well! I don't know exactly what I said, but I do remember thinking, "Duh!" (although I don't think we said, "duh" in those days). Well, of course I'm born again—have been for some time—actually since my Baptism, but lots of Christians don't quite understand that!

What I did say was, "Why do you think that?" He said, I can tell by the way you talk. So . . . I was in! I was now declared "born again" by the evangelical pastor of Grace Community Church! (Just an aside. I haven't worn a clerical collar in the last 35 years. The Lutheran Church is the evangelical catholic church, and I identify more with the evangelical side.)

Also in Burney was the wonderful hospitality of Burney Presbyterian Church. It was there that we held worship. And it was there that for $25 a month, we could do whatever we wanted as long as we were the first ones to hold a place on the calendar. They were to us a very generous part of the one holy Christian and apostolic Church.

The next major insight I had into the Body of Christ happened while at my next call, St. John's in Napa. Again, I was drawn to a prayer meeting with pastors of other denominations. One of them was a really fine Baptist pastor. As we were meeting together, he opened his Bible and read a verse. My observation (previously mentioned) was, "Hey—he's using our Bible!" (I told you I was a bit narrow-minded.) My learning was that just as there is one holy Christian and apostolic church, so there is also one Bible. Of course, I know this is obvious, but this was an insight God needed to give me along the way to truly understanding the whole of the Church.

Then, while I was still maturing in understanding, not a lot happened. My only memory of pastors getting together at my next call, was a big disagreement I had with a more liberal pastor of another denomination. I felt quite strongly that our ministerial fellowship should be distinctively Christian. He didn't.

Church of Modesto

Then an amazing thing happened. The church and school in Brea continued to grow and were doing well. I received a call to Grace, Modesto, and off we went to our fourth church. The first month I was there, there was an interesting article in the paper about sex. I wrote my first letter to the editor of the Modesto Bee. A few days later, I went to the ministerial association, and met Pastor Joel (real name), who became a good friend of mine.

When I met Joel he commented on my letter to the editor. Then he said, "You know a friend of mine said there needed to be a letter in response to the same article." Joel answered him that I had already written one and it had been published. His friend said, "Well a letter from a Lutheran really doesn't count." Welcome to the one holy Christian and apostolic Church in Modesto.

God, also, was not too keen on church relations there. Then . . .

In the fall of 1993, I received an invitation to attend the first four day prayer summit sponsored by the ministerial association and led by Northwest Renewal Ministries and Multnomah College. My thought was, "Four days?" My second thought was that I wasn't going to let the rest of the pastors (50 went) do something that I wasn't part of.

The prayer summit, of course, was a blessing, and the beginning of what would be soon be called "The Church of Modesto." At the end of the summit, the leader said that this was only the beginning, that what was needed was weekly prayer on the part of all the participants. I never saw so many pastors looking so uncomfortable, and muttering all sorts of things about time, schedules and other things that pastors are inclined to believe are important. Then one pastor got out his pocket calendar, and a couple more followed suit.

The time was set for one hour at noon on Wednesdays at First Baptist downtown. For the rest of my time in Modesto, I had the privilege of being, with the other pastors in town, an associate pastor of the Church of Modesto. We had about 80 participants praying each week and attending the annual prayer summits in January.

This was a great example of the Body of Christ—one holy Christian and apostolic Church, recognizing who it was and how it was connected. One of the results of continuing prayer for revival, was the coming to Modesto of the play, "Heaven's Gates and Hell's Flames," at Calvary Temple. Subsequently called "The Miracle in Modesto," 80,000 people attended "The Play," as it was called all over town. This, in a community of about 170,000 at that time.

Virtually every church received new members as a result of 25,000 first time or recommitments to Christ!

One of my close friends in The Church of Modesto was Pastor Ross. Ross was a pastor, but also a businessman, owning a recreational business in town. As a result, Ross would get free lift tickets and take me skiing. It gave us a chance to get to know each other and invariably part of our conversation would be about the Body of Christ. We explored each other's church background and distinctive church teachings.

On one trip up the ski lift I said to Ross, "You know, the people I grew up with would be surprised that I had a friend who was a "Holy Roller." Ross said that he understood, because if the people he grew up with knew he was talking to a Lutheran, they would have thought he had gone off the deep end. The road of not understanding the fullness of the one holy Christian and apostolic Church goes both ways.

And my belief that the Body of Christ is one was considerably strengthened by my Church of Modesto experience.

Then on to Tempe, Arizona. My first thought, of course, was to recreate the Church of Modesto in Tempe. You know, though, God is in charge and has different plans for different places. There were good prayer experiences and good pastor friends, but the next chapter in my part of the one holy Christian and apostolic Church was at Gethsemane.

When I arrived, I discovered that there was Phoenix Mar Thomas Congregation (East Indian, evangelical/ecumenical church—Mar Thomas translates "Saint Thomas," *the* St. Thomas (doubting), who is credited with first bringing the gospel to India in the first century A.D.) worshipping periodically in our sanctuary. Would this be O.K. with me?

Remembering the Presbyterians in Burney, and just fresh from my Church of Modesto experience, I was, of course, delighted to have our facilities used by another church.

Next came St. Thomas Orthodox Church of India—they were a lot like us, but their use of incense was disconcerting the next morning! Then came a Bible Church from India. At this point I noted that America was not the only place with different denominations in the one holy Christian and apostolic Church! Our buildings were more and more used for worship by the Body of Christ.

Then one day two men and one woman showed up. Would it be O.K. for them to have a look around at our facilities. They needed to find a place for their Bible Church (American) to worship. Our family life center (gym, kitchen, offices) had just been built. I showed them around, emphasizing the Sunday evening/afternoon availability of our sanctuary. They left.

A few days later they came back with their pastor and another church leader. This time they wouldn't let me show them the sanctuary—only the gym and some classrooms. They were also interested in offices. Tempe Bible Church became the fifth church using our facilities—noting that we had buildings and others needed a place for worship and making disciples in the one holy Christian and apostolic Church.

This was a blessing in my life and others, as, indeed is the One Holy Christian and Apostolic Church the Body of Christ!

Chapter Nine

Commandments Five and Six

Issues of Life and Death

One of my greatest joys in ministry was teaching *Christian Basics*. *Christian Basics* was (call it what you will) "Pastor's Class," "Adult Instruction," "Adult Confirmation Class," "Christianity 101." I called it *Christian Basics* and I taught it about 100 times during my 36 years of full-time pastoral ministry. I used several different time frames, but discovered that Sundays before or after worship worked the best. When I had two services and lay teachers for other classes, I did it in between. After I had three services, I did it after the third service. When I got home, Nancy had Sunday dinner (like in the Midwest) waiting, and then a nap!

I'm not going to say much about this adult instruction class, except on two of the commandments, which, in the United States today, need to be addressed. I saved discussion of the Ten Commandments for the last weeks of the class and called them Christian Living I, loving God first (with a separate hour on prayer and worship), and Christian Living II, loving neighbor as self.

I would introduce the law as civil, ceremonial, and moral. I would talk about the law as a curb, mirror, and guide, and then say "We will use it in all three ways, but let's concentrate on its usefulness in guiding the way we live." Yes, I know that's an arguable point, but then, in this case I'm the teacher!

After the first four commandments, putting God first, taking care of His name, being careful to rest and worship, and honoring parents and recognizing authority, we would get to "You shall not kill." What does this mean?

May I just put in a quick paragraph on Commandment seven: specifically wrestling with honesty and our attitude towards money, including stewardship. These are huge subjects that can be accessed in many other places.

5th Commandment—I would ask "What are the life and death issues in life?" As the class, which was no longer intimidated this 7th week, offered suggestions, I'd write them on the board and make sure they included war, capital punishment, abortion, euthanasia, murder, suicide, and artificial prolonging of life. Then this is what I taught.

War and capital punishment are decisions that belong to the kingdom on the left—government. Those decisions need to be made there. Obviously there is a great deal more discussion needed on this point, but that is for another time and place.

Suicide is wrong, but not the unforgivable sin. We do not get saved by being without sin, and neither, in my opinion, are we lost because the last moment in our lives is committing a sinful act. Think of the believing Christian guy who has an abusive argument with his wife, storms out of the house, and gets killed by an oncoming train. One doesn't lose his or her salvation if he or she dies without confessing the most recent sin.

My dad (very conservative Lutheran pastor), was not at all sure that a person committing suicide would (could?) be saved, but would tell the story that he once had the Christian service for a person who committed suicide because the man did so because he was afraid he

---

would freeze to death that winter. On his porch was stacked a great deal of firewood. Dad simply said the man was not in his right mind. One truly wonders if any suicidal person is in his or her right mind.

Then I would tell the class that we definitely were a pro-life church. Birth control is accepted, but once there is a pregnancy, there is a living human being in the womb. Easy to understand—the fetus is living—it is growing—non-living things do not grow. It is human, what else can it be? He/she has a unique DNA, and is developing into a soon-to-be human baby living outside the womb! Killing the baby before it's born is against the 5th Commandment. Exceptions? Probably to save the life (not health) (also rare) of the mother. Rape and incest (same as rape)? I personally am against aborting the baby—adoption would be a good choice. However, in the rare likelihood of this occurrence, a very prayerful decision needs to be made. Certainly the church is here for support of any kind.

Murder—obviously wrong. Jesus said it includes hate. Think about that!

Euthanasia? God is the One who determines when life begins (conception), and when life ends. We simply are not to engage in mercy killing, in whatever form it might take. On the other hand, I believe the artificial prolonging of life is also wrong.

I'm not sure I ever put this in writing, but when it comes to this subject, I have said, "If you want to die, don't go to a hospital; they won't let you die!" Now, I know that is somewhat of a misrepresentation, but it is heartbreaking to see someone kept artificially alive, for whatever reason, when actually without the ventilator or feeding tube, without other artificial means, this life would be ended. Having said that, I know very well, that there are dozens, maybe hundreds, of scenarios that could be discussed.

Just two situations I have witnessed. But before those, one time, and I'm sure readers could all tell of something similar, a patient on major life-support came through the treatment and recovered. I'm sure that is always the goal. However, often times these heroic efforts simply prolong life and put the person through prolonged suffering.

Sometimes it happens even though there is a "do not resuscitate" order. I was called to the hospital very late one evening. Herb was someone with whom I had been in a small group Bible study. He was on dialysis, but always in good spirits. I don't remember exactly why the paramedics were called, but they hooked Herb up before there were black and white instructions found, which indicated otherwise. His wife, Helen, very much aware of what was going on, decided to keep him on the ventilator until the family arrived. Herb was not awake.

After everyone had a chance to say goodbye, Helen said to me, "It's time." By then all was in order that there was no question Herb could be freed from his artificial life. Helen and I went to speak to the doctor. He was so very kind, and compassionately spoke of what the consequences would be of disconnecting the ventilator. He used such caring language that finally I interrupted and said, "Doctor, Helen knows exactly what you are saying, and she understands what will happen." With that, Herb was released and went home to be with Jesus!

Another time, when I was in one of my "He never should have gone to the hospital" moods, another caring doctor captured my attention. Dan had a major heart attack. Again, the diligent paramedics hooked him up and took him to the hospital where he lay in the intensive care unit for several days. His wife, Dorothy, said to me and others, "Dan simply is not here any longer—he's gone." But his body was being kept alive, much to my dismay.

I was there the afternoon that the doctor spoke to the family.

I had great respect for what he said, and I then pondered whether I was too harsh in my critical statement that "they won't let you die in the hospital." The doctor lovingly said that the initial hope was that something could be done for Dan, but they were now convinced they had tried everything. Dorothy was quite relieved when Dan's body was allowed to pass away, since he wasn't there anyway!

Now something about one of the finest ministries (although be it not distinctively Christian, but certainly is there for Christians from a Christian perspective) I have observed. It is hospice care.

My first encounter was during the earlier years of my pastoring, when I was called to the home of two of our active members. Ken had died, and the hospice worker phoned me and asked me to come over. Ken's body was still in the home, but he was obviously dead. Alice, his wife, of course was in tears.

The hospice worker said, "Would you like some tea?" Not very smart, I thought that was a strange question. Alice said "No thank you." I also said that I didn't care for any. With that, the lady said, "Well I would; I'll make some!" And I was introduced to hospice, with its fine training and wonderfully qualified personnel. She, of course, was right on, giving a gentle, but firm acclamation that Ken might be dead, but the rest of us were not, and a bit of tea might help in this mournful situation.

Then, she spoke again. In the far distance sirens were faintly heard. She said, "You're not going to like what happens next, but even though we know that Ken is dead, they are required to come with their sirens on." Over the years I have continued to appreciate the hospice lady who was there that day.

You need to know that what comes next is my personal observation, and may not necessarily be philosophically accurate from a hospice professional point of view.

The first time I met Joyce I had just taken a call to a new congregation. I was sitting at a desk (not my own) in the church office. Joyce, a very active member, came into the office and saw me sitting there. Being a bit abrupt, but very comfortable around the church, she looked at me and said, "And who are you?" I said, "I'm the new pastor." Without missing a beat, she said, "Then come and give me a hug!" And so we were introduced.

A few months later, we were at a meeting together. Recognizing her skills and church connections, I had asked that she be included on the building team. She came to the meeting that night, with a grandchild whom she was babysitting. Someone served cake—I was liking this church more and more. Her grandchild accidentally knocked his/her (don't remember now) cake onto the floor. Joyce didn't pick it up. I thought that was very strange for a competent grandmother.

A few days later, I knew why. Joyce had a brain tumor. She had surgery, but rapidly declined. It was the end of the Joyce we all knew—now there was a very nice lady, but one who needed constant support just to walk.

Hospice care was engaged for Joyce. She was cared for at home with a lot of help from her family. One Sunday afternoon, some of the guys from our men's chorus went over to sing for her. She, of course, was delighted. This was close to, if not, the last group of visitors. I learned that in the next day or two, Joyce's pain medication would be increased to the point that she would no longer be awake. Since there were no heroic efforts (including intravenous fluid administration), Joyce would not be receiving liquids and she was expected to die within three or four days.

I remember being somewhat shocked. I had not thought through all of this at that time in my life and sincerely wondered if this were moral. I don't wonder that any more. I believe we err too often in prolonging life artificially. God is to decide when a person's life comes to an end. Prolonging it artificially is not ours to do. Allowing someone to rest comfortably, without pain, in my opinion, is natural.

As the years went by and I became more and more familiar with hospice care, I became aware of a wonderful hospice facility in our neighborhood. I was always pleased to find out that someone's loved one, who was close to death, was there. The person was easy to visit, the family did not have the trauma of the person dying in the living room (although some chose that instead), I knew the person would be well cared for, and I knew that death would be allowed to come in a most compassionate way. Thank you hospice!

Joan chose to have her dying husband at home, with hospice care there. She had several children, and it seemed someone, even young grandchildren, was there day after day. Joan was someone I had known from a previous congregation, where she was the church secretary. Her husband, Bob, was known to be quite outspoken, and certainly "in charge" around the house. It was strange to have him lying quietly in the living room while the kids were rambunctious.

We were in the process of building a columbarium at our church. Each time I visited Bob, Joan asked me how it was coming, how much it was going to cost, and told me she wanted to contribute something. I assured her that it would be done soon, so that Bob's cremaines could be placed there. After his death, Joan came over with a $10,000 check towards the columbarium. She "just knew" that God wanted her to do this. So she did! She and her family were there for the dedication of the columbarium.

All about Sex
(OK a Few Things about Sex)

One of the Ten Commandments that is so relevant today (not that the others aren't) is "You shall not commit adultery." That is so clear, so obvious, and it has many ramifications. Where to begin?

First of all a list of sexual topics that are, in my opinion, included in this commandment. I'll just list them, and then write about them. Any sexual contact with another person outside of marriage, including: adultery, pre-marital sex, fornication, casual sex, homosexual actions. Pornography doesn't involve another person, I don't think, but it surely is not something a person wants to be involved in.

I believe that sex outside of marriage is the number one social problem in America today. I have stated that publicly in our local newspaper, and privately with friends and families members. And for sure from the pulpit! I have had people argue with me, and state that there are other social problems that are higher on the problem list. However, I stand by my statement, since a great deal of poverty and a great deal of crime are the direct result of sex outside of marriage.

It is not hard to find articles reporting that the number one thing male prisoners have in common is the lack of a loving relationship with their fathers. This supersedes education, race, age, and economic circumstances. Having a father in the home is a major influence in the moral development of a boy, and undoubtedly a girl as well. Nothing is better for a child than living in a home where his or her parents are married to one another.

Let me digress for a moment regarding marriage. When I addressed people in our congregation on the issue of marriage, I would say two things: 1) If you are married, stay married. Do whatever it takes to have a loving, committed marital relationship. And . .

. since I mentioned love, when it comes to the marriage relationship, I am on the side of commitment being more important than feelings. I would tell couples that in pre-marriage counseling and in wedding sermons.

2) Divorce is not the unforgivable sin (the sin against the Holy Spirit, of which one never repents, is). If you are divorced, and unable to re-establish a relationship with your spouse, repent of your divorce and know that you are forgiven. Yes, I did marry divorced people to another person. However . . . if I married a person the first time, I wouldn't the second. And, true confessions, one time I made a mistake in agreeing to marry someone. I simply didn't do the right thing, but at the time it seemed as though it was.

Not having pre-marital sex precludes several problems. In our time, there are any number of people who have been hurt by divorce. This is one of the reasons that people are living together before marriage. I'm sure that at least one example pops up in the mind of every person reading this. And . . . I'm also quite sure that many people reading this can name one or more situations where people have been together for several years and it all seems just fine. And . . . I have to admit that sometimes it seems to me also that an ongoing live-in relationship, especially one where the couple is raising a child of their own, appears to be working. Except there is always the possibility of just splitting and ending it.

God's way is marriage. I used to tell the kids in confirmation class (when they were 13 and still not involved) 1) education first, 2) marriage second, 3) sex third, 4) don't marry someone who is not a Christian (or willing to accept the Lord), and 5) don't marry someone your parents tell you not to. Now I realize that this advice may be imperfect, but the more young people who take it, the better their lives will be.

Pre-marital sex can be hurtful in several different ways, including major trauma when the marriage doesn't take place. One or the other or both are wounded and wondering how a true marital relationship can ever be there for them.

Both partners saving sex for marriage also eliminates pregnancy out of marriage, potentially unwanted children, sexually transmitted diseases (including AIDS), and the possibility of abortion. Fornication—including one-night-stands is even more problematic, especially with the health issues. Casual sex is not what God intends!

Then there is the matter of homosexuality. This is particularly challenging in our society today. The most exasperating part of the discussion is the lack of clarity. The way I like to say it is, "You don't have to be gay, just because you are gay." There is a great deal of confusion about the difference between being attracted to the same sex and living a gay lifestyle. One doesn't have to follow the other.

At the same time there is a great deal of confusion as to the cause of homosexuality. Popular in our culture is the term "born gay." And . . . this certainly appears to be the case for those who are gay. They did not choose to be gay, it happened to them. However . . . it is not genetic, although genetics may play a role.

I went to a "Love Won Out" conference, sponsored by Focus on the Family Ministries. It was responsibly explained that in between the age of 18 months and 3 years, boys need to shift from identifying with their mothers to identifying with their fathers. When this doesn't happen, the process of "male-longing" begins, and that turns sexual later in life. This was not chosen. (The sexual identity for girls is a little more complicated because it involves not only their relationship with their mothers, but with their perceived identity with friends as well.)

Sexual orientation is not chosen, but what one does with it, is. Orientation doesn't change, but a person has a choice of what to do about it. I don't have to say much about the demands of the gay lobbyists today; it's all over the news. I do have to say that there are thousands of gay men who are happily married to the opposite sex and are fulfilled with their family life. As one of these happily married guys said to a group of us, "And . . . in addition to loving my wife and being loved by her, I am spared continually being distracted by good-looking women."

Please see the story of a happily married gay man coming next.

Chapter Ten

Someone Who's Gay

You don't have to be gay. I realize this statement is controversial, but let me explain. The thesis for this chapter is, "You don't have to be gay just because you are gay." There is a big difference between homosexual orientation, and homosexual action. This chapter is a glimpse of what it's like to be attracted to the same sex instead of the opposite sex. It is the story of a homosexual person who lives a heterosexual life. I will call him Neal. I have his permission to tell his story, but not to reveal his identity.

Neal was born into a Christian family, and has been an active part of a church. In his childhood Neal didn't realize he was gay and probably didn't even know such an orientation existed. He just was, so he thought, like everyone else, looking forward to the future, and someday being the dad instead of the kid. Of course, in high school, his understanding of sex broadened, but he still didn't figure this out.

What did happen, however, was that over the years he developed crushes on guys his age. Thinking about it, Neal called them boyfriends. There were seven of them, and almost an eighth (but he knew better by then) over a twelve year period. The dynamics were pretty much the same, and there never was any physical contact, nor even any revealing of the "I'm in love with you" aspects of the crush.

What there was, was a real admiration for the person, and a desire to spend as much time with him as possible. There were even times when they went on double dates together, no one realizing that Neal was really more interested in his boyfriend than the girl he was with. The crushes happened twice in high school and twice in college. By college Neal began to have an understanding of his sexual orientation. A story in an English class about a young man who liked to see bare chested, sun-tanned guys got him to thinking.

Some time later, realizing that he once again, "was in love with a guy," he took note of a muscular male in an in-between class study area, who was sitting across the table from him. Not being able to stand this attraction any longer, he walked in tears across campus to the Christian student center where he went to church. The pastor, whose role was counseling, was in his office. This was the beginning of the next part of Neal's story—counselors.

Except for a friend, who was totally appalled, this pastor was the first person to whom Neal expressed his inner-turmoil. As it turned out, Neal felt better having told his secret to someone, but the pastor was of very little help. He assured Neal that he wasn't gay (why he thought that, Neal could never understand), and sent him on his not-so-merry way.

Then came graduate school, and boyfriend number five. Once again, Neal decided he needed counseling. It was a campus with two identified psychologists. Neal chose the good-looking one. It turned out he didn't do counseling, just instruction, so Neal went off to see the other one. This professor was very much interested in counseling Neal and met with him several times. When it was suggested that Neal join a therapy group, he decided that the counselor had been a big help (and he had) and he certainly was not willing to expose his homosexuality to other students, he declined and declared himself much better. And he was.

However, regardless of consideration, and regardless (at least in this case) of prayer, one doesn't stop one's homosexual orientation.

Neal decided that this was a "thorn in the flesh," and God's grace was sufficient. And largely that was true.

Sometime later Neal fell in love again. This time two things happened. He told the guy that he was in love with him. The response was, "Well what are you going to do about it?" What Neal did was to see his third counselor. Once again there was a release of tension, just being able to share with someone. The counselor was helpful, but made it clear that Neal was not to "come out of the closet;" he was not to tell anyone.

Time passed. At an off-campus 12 week training seminar, there was opportunity to engage still another counselor, Neal's mentor. This was when he found himself watching an unusually attractive (so Neal thought) young man in a dining facility. Neal told his mentor. The mentor said he wasn't at all surprised, and that while he should not have any sexual contact with a man, it was perfectly fine to enjoy the good looks of the kid in the dining hall.

Internship. Last "boyfriend." Nothing more, according to Neal, to report.

During these years Neal would date girls, but never found the right one. However, wanting to be in love, get married, and have children, Neal persisted, and found the female love of his life. Long story short, Neal, still noticing good-looking guys, is happily married with children, and has a great family life!

So . . . one might wonder, how many non-counselors know of Neal's sexual orientation? The first person mentioned — never talked about again, although he and Neal were friends a long time. Also — the one Neal told he loved, who was still a friend when he (the guy) got married. Then . . . no one until years later when he shared this with a colleague, who was very understanding. Then . . .

Neal was at a Christian retreat. Due to the closeness of the event, Neal decided to share his secret with a couple of the men. They were very understanding, and one was very supportive over the next few years. When Neal was moving to a new location, he took him out to lunch and told him how grateful he was that he had not written him off as a friend. His friend said to Neal, "On the contrary, it was a great compliment to me that you trusted me with your conflict."

When Neal told these men his secret, he asked whether he should tell the entire group at the retreat. Together both of them shouted, "NO!" This reaction brings me to the last point of this chapter.

There's something that, out of compassion and concern, bothers me a great deal about the way our culture handles homosexuality. O.K.—it is more than just one thing.

1) First of all it is the lack of clarity when homosexuality is talked about. The distinction between orientation and putting that orientation into practice is totally obscured. There is a very big difference in being attracted, which is not chosen, and having same-sex relations, which is chosen. The church ought to be a loud voice whenever the opportunity arises, to declare this distinction; and also to be an encouragement to people with a homosexual orientation, letting them know they have a choice. Again, there are many, many homosexually oriented persons who have a great life living a heterosexual lifestyle, complete with marriage and child raising.

2) The homosexual person simply cannot, for the most part, come out of the closet. I suppose this has a lot to do with (again the distinction) what coming out of the closet means. Is it admitting to a homosexual life-style, or is it revealing the struggle within? Why can't this be honestly discussed? And why can't a person share this with his or her family and friends without recrimination? Not being able to share this major part of one's life is isolating and lonely.

3) The ramifications of letting others know one's orientation, especially when one is endeavoring to help people understand. If this were able to be openly discussed from a Christian point of view,

understanding law, gospel, forgiveness, and God's love in life no matter who one is, I believe society would be benefited, many more people would understand, and the homosexual person would experience love and support so very superior to facing his/her orientation alone. I also think that support from the heterosexual world would decrease the number of gays who feel they can only be happy in having a transitory or permanent same-sex relationship.

Chapter Eleven

Odds and Ends

Words

My favorite word in the English language is grace. Grace is defined two different ways, both with the same meaning. I grew up understanding that grace was God's undeserved love. More recently, I've heard it defined as God's unmerited favor. Put them together and these descriptive phrases quite nicely explain that the blessings come at God's pleasure, not on our own.

My second favorite English word is compassion. I don't think compassion needs explanation—well putting it into practice might take some encouragement—but the word compassion is quite understood on its own.

There are words, however, with which I have struggled over the years. These are words that are often used when talking about things in the Christian understanding of life and our relationship with God. I have come up with definitions that hopefully, succinctly make the words understandable and useful.

The first is faith. There is the common teaching that faith is knowing, believing and trusting what the Bible tells us of our relationship with God. This, of course, is helpful.

When I talk about faith I like to define it as a trusting relationship.

We are saved by grace, through faith. Ephesians 2:8-9 is so clear on this. Next to John 3:16, it is, in my opinion, the most important verse to let us know how we are able to have a relationship with God. It is through the death and resurrection of Jesus Christ, God's Son, Savior and Lord. It is *by* grace, but comes to us *through* faith—a trusting relationship created in our hearts by the Holy Spirit who calls us to this trusting relationship—faith—through the gospel—the good news of Jesus' life, death, and resurrection for the sins of the world.

One word that I have had a hard time getting easily into my head is righteousness. Now I realize what I'm about to say could be refined, even challenged, because I don't think it covers the entire use of the word. However, my definition of righteousness is, "what we need in our hearts to be right with God." Again, it is something God does for us through repentance, leading to faith.

As long as I wrote "repentance," suffice it to say that the word repentance simply means turning around and going another direction. Surely we also commonly use it as an expression of sorrow for sin, and change in general. But it does mean to stop and go the other way.

Witness is another word that I believe needs an understandable definition if people are going to do it! There is perhaps no word that is more intimidating for Christians, than the word witness. And then to top it off, Jesus encourages (instructs) us in the first chapter of Acts to be His witnesses. What to do?

I have come to the conclusion that if a person is to witness, he or she is simply to tell what they know when they have a chance. I don't know where or when that might be, whether with family or acquaintances, or with total strangers. The best time, of course, is when someone asks a spiritual question. How far does one go? One stops telling what he or she knows when the other person stops listening. It does no good to continue on. Tell what you know when you have a chance.

The last word for which I came up with a definition, is glory. Actually, for years I wondered exactly what glory means, and even now I'm not totally sure. I do know, however, that it describes God, and it is other than what we ordinarily experience in our lives. So I looked it up, and I looked it up again, and was never quite satisfied. However, determined to have a definition that could be shared, I finally came to the conclusion that my definition for glory is "exalted honor." That works for me. However, even as that is said, I think that there needs to be some glowing bright light associated with this exalted honor!

Preaching

I was 34 years old, and had just taken a call to my first solo pastorate in a congregation of size. Previously I had served as a worker-priest in a congregation of nine families—we had lots of seminary graduates that year and any congregation who wanted a pastor could have one, even if the pastor had to make his own living.

After that I was an associate pastor in a great congregation, which had a school. I learned a lot there, which turned out to be very useful since I was in congregations with schools for 34 of my 36 years of pre-retirement pastoring. We arrived in the Napa Valley with no children, and left 4 ½ year later with three! Miriam was only three weeks old when we were at worship in our new church. It was the morning of my installation.

Pastor O had been the vacancy pastor for a year. They liked him and gave him tickets to Germany for his farewell gift. He led worship that morning. He was easy to listen to. He told several stories of past pastoral experiences during the message. That wasn't my preaching style—I did lots of studying of the text and subscribed to a sermon-illustration magazine.

When we got home, gazing about our new house and entertaining children who had just moved, leaving everything familiar behind, we commented on the sermon. Nancy astutely stated that older pastors preached a whole lot different from younger ones— they had a life time of stories to tell. Now I do too!

Sometime later I was at our circuit pastors' meeting—it was a great circuit—I always enjoyed meeting with those guys. There was an older (80ish) pastor there, whom they had invited to share some things. He was asked if he were still preaching, and if so, what he did to prepare. Was he using any special sermon preparation aids? I got the impression that he was one of the pastors in that area respected for his sermons. The 80-something pastor got a twinkle in his eye and said, "Yes, I use both the Bible and the dictionary—very helpful!"

At the time I thought, "Wow—who could ever use only the Bible and dictionary?" I thought about his comment over the years. One of the blessings of getting to retirement age is that I have discovered that indeed, all one needs at this age is the Bible and the dictionary. Oh—now Google is also useful!

This might be a good place to tell one of the most wonderful things that ever happened to me while preaching. My last congregation was great! We had a sanctuary that was too small. It was wider than it was long, so we were very close to one another. I preached from the front of the chancel, which also was close. We laughed together and cried together. These were wonderful people of the Lord!

One Sunday I said something that was not planned (actually, that would happen a bit too often). What I said about a verse was,

"The Bible didn't get it quite right here." Dumb. And misspoken. The congregation let out a very audible gasp, and looked horrified. It was a wonderful experience for me to realize that they did listen, and they had discernment.

I said, "Let me rephrase that." And I continued, "This is a passage that is somewhat difficult to understand." They looked relieved. And then I continued to explain how wonderful what just happened was. I told them that indeed it was their responsibility to listen to what the pastor was saying and to check that it was always in accord with Scripture. I was blessed!

Mistakes

As I write about mistakes I've made, I know there are a lot more of them than are coming to mind at this time. I think the ones I remember all have to do with offending people. And even there, with my personality, I'm sure I've offended many more people than I remember. I am really good at apologizing. Mistakes . . .

Matt's mother and sister were faithful attendees at worship. But Matt wasn't. I think he got confirmed, but don't remember for sure. His sister went into full time ministry. One Sunday teenage Matt came to church with his mother. They sat fairly close to the front, and I spotted Matt with a cap on. A wiser pastor would have rejoiced that Matt was there and ignored the hat. Not me. I went over and asked him to not wear a hat in church. He never came back. Major mistake.

One time I was in the lobby of the church office which was also the lobby of the school office. One of the most helpful and reliable members of the church, who had a daughter in our school, was also there. Something not involving her (the mom) didn't go right that morning. I complained about the undependable nature of volunteers.

This great lady came storming across the lobby and told me that this place wouldn't even exist without the volunteers and I had better never say anything like that again. I didn't. Ever again!

Over the years I probably communed a handful of people I perhaps shouldn't have. That, however, in my opinion, wasn't a mistake (unless I didn't follow up). What I remember as a mistake was the time or two that someone inadvertently came to the communion table not understanding the parameters of our communion policy, and I gave them a blessing instead of the sacrament. They, like Matt, didn't come back again.

The biggest mistake I made was something I thought was a good idea, but it wasn't. It didn't turn out. About three years before retirement, I read a book about the importance of Small Groups. I had always thought they were important, and actually had written a Small Group Manual for a class in my doctorate studies.

At that point, I decided that I was going to put all my effort into Small Group ministry—we called them Life Circles. I started by training the first leaders. I think we started with this one Small Group. Then we had four, then nine, and I think over twelve. At that point, the going thing (there's always "the latest" in the Christian community) was a video lecture series, with dinner and table discussion.

I compelled all our Small Groups to come to this, and recruit non-Small Group participants for their Small Groups. All I need to say is that even though people were blessed by the video series, and even by the table discussion, this was a dismal failure—a major mistake. At the end there were fewer Life Circles than when the videos started.

Transitioning from traditional ministry to Small Groups only, didn't work in our case. However, I do want to say to readers, that that doesn't mean it can't happen. I believe it is the biblical model.

Voters Assembly

Ah, the Voters Assembly! I absolutely believe in congregational autonomy. Take a look at the Church over the ages. Take a look at many denominations today. Take a look at many congregations today. Authority, in my opinion, leads to arrogance and leads to lots of meetings, retreats, and even well-meaning strategies, that really are not the biblical model of the Church. I believe that bishops, overseers, are local, not regional. That is not to say there's no place for coordination, but the real church is local.

And that brings us to Voters Assemblies—congregational meetings. Voters Assemblies have a place. Only the congregational assembly is to perform four functions of the congregation. 1) Elect officers, 2) Adopt the budget, 3) Call church workers, and 4) Authorize the construction of buildings. All other church business needs to be done by smaller teams/committees. Voters Assemblies, properly understood, have a vital ministry function in the congregation. However . . .

All too often, Voters Assemblies seem to provide the opportunity for dissension. Of particular concern to me is the fact (at least in my experience) that voters meetings are places that anyone at almost any time (if there's a non-authoritative chairperson—and because of the loving nature of the church, most go overboard to be nice) can get up and say whatever he or she wants, regardless of the veracity of the content.

My hardest task at Voters, was keeping my mouth shut. Yet there was time after time, when I knew what the person was saying was not factual. It's not easy being a pastor at Voters Assembly. Enough said.

Getting things Done

What does it take to get things done, to make things happen in the local church? What it doesn't take are teams or committees, elected or not, saying, "We should." This takes place over and over again, sometimes for weeks, sometimes for years.

One night one of my favorite guys (who once agreed with me that if you go to school and did what they said long enough, you could also have a doctorate—his was a PhD in Engineering) said, "Pastor John you are always three or four months ahead of the rest of us." I took it as a compliment. The truth, in my opinion, is that visionary leadership needs to be thinking ahead. Sometimes not just a few months, but a few years.

One of the positive things we did in the congregations I served was annual leadership retreats. They included faith and relationship building. They also included setting annual, two, and five year goals. And then just for the fun of it—ten year goals. It was interesting to see which of the ten year goals would become five or two or even one year goals the next time around.

One of my observations (after a few years of wanting stuff to happen that didn't) was that it never hurts to talk about something that needs to be done in the future. The first time it is mentioned, people look very skeptical, sometimes wishful, every so often appalled! However, a year later, there would be nodding heads. And not too many years later the building would be dedicated, or the new staff person in place. Ministries, such as Stephen Ministry, could be in place even sooner—and adding a grade a year to the school. Having the pastor mention a need often enough gets the idea in people's minds and then when it's time, with a leader and a date, to take a vote, it can happen! I've seen it many times!

One time I felt a change in plans was truly needed. The

congregation had been talking about a new sanctuary for years—in fact it was one of the first things I learned about the church when the principal gave me a tour of the campus and showed me . . . "and this is the fellowship hall, in which we are worshipping until the new sanctuary is built." "When?" I asked, looking around to see if we could really play basketball in this space. "Hasn't been decided yet."

I love to build buildings that are useful for the Kingdom. Even though there were already 19 classrooms, a gym, and two new office configurations built during my time at previous congregations, I had never had the privilege of being the pastor to dedicate a new sanctuary. This was one (but hopefully not the primary) reason I accepted the call.

After I was at this church and school for a while, it became apparent to me that what we needed more than a new sanctuary (we already had one, although truly it was a temporary situation), was a Family Life Center. I went to the annual planning meeting ready to share this. I actually went with apprehension, since I knew it was the congregation's dream to have a new sanctuary. In fact, we had a building fund with the expectation that we would be building one soon.

The leadership team listened to what I had to say and agreed that it made sense. Presenting to the congregation was more difficult, but they reluctantly said, "Yes!" We lost one family, and one of the guys I most highly valued was very disappointed.

The Family Life Center turned out great—the youth room was too small, but that was later rectified with a remodel. The rest was top-notch. Probably the best kitchen in our church body. And . . . we had plenty of worship space on Christmas Eve and Easter Sunday— made sure we had a great portable stage. Great building!

And . . . I asked my disappointed guy what he thought, and he said that he was good with it. The new sanctuary? When I left, it was designed, and had several hundred thousand in the bank ready to go. Which brings me to the next point about getting things done.

Person and Date on the Calendar

During the course of being a pastor I began to notice what it took to get things done. One of the first things I noticed was that a woman with the spiritual gift of administration would always make sure her area of ministry was in order. One of them single-handedly got the Altar Guild functioning in a most marvelous fashion. Others, too, can do this.

The second thing I figured out was that as long as people said, "We should . . ." It never happened. What is needed is a time frame.

I ended up with the understanding that anything (that God is in favor of) can be accomplished (relatively easily) if there are two starters. First is a person who truly wants to see this happen and is willing to provide initial leadership. Second is a date. The project will always be "we should" until there is a date on the calendar for the first meaningful meeting. Then there will be an installation or dedication or an improved Sunday School. Praise God for those initiators and getting the date of the first meeting on the calendar.

Chapter Twelve

Most Important Verses

I have to believe I was one of the most learned Lutheran kids ever to study Luther's Small Catechism. However, I never went to Lutheran Grade School (as did my mom and dad, my aunts and uncles, my wife, and my children), so this might not at all be true!

What I do know is that the year we moved to a small, rural congregation, my dad discovered there were fewer than five 7th and 8th graders for Saturday morning Confirmation Classes, and announced that all children of the congregation in grades five to eight would be attending class. I was in 5th grade! Consequently, I diligently went through the "1943 Catechism," "Luther's Small Catechism" with "A short explanation" (331 questions and answers supported by 703 Bible verses) published by Concordia Publishing House, four times. I faithfully memorized at least 600 (some repeats) of those verses—maybe more!

It would be good if Christians today knew at least fifty Bible passages by memory, but that doesn't seem to be the case. So during my final years in full time ministry, I wrote an article for the church newsletter, "If you only know five," and the next month, "If you want to know five more." I listed the most important (in my estimation) Bible passages and encouraged the congregation to memorize them, including location. They are . . .

First Five

Of course John 3:16 is at the top of the list. We live in a day and age where John 3:16 has been prominently displayed in several ways at sporting events. This is the declaration of God's love for the world and the prescription for salvation. God gave His Son, Jesus the Christ, so that through a relationship with Him, there is eternal life. Where one spends eternity (with or apart from God), depends on this faith relationship.

Two: Romans 6:23 elaborates on this concept. Left on our own, the ravages of sin end up in death—and eternal death, i.e. eternal separation from God who gave His Son that this not happen. But God gives the gift of eternal life through the death and resurrection of Jesus. Quite a contrast. No wonder this verse is among the top five.

Three: Ephesians 2:8-9. I like to think of this as the most Lutheran verse in the Bible. Surely other evangelical churches love it as well, but in my opinion, Lutherans are the ones who understand it the best. True—Lutherans have some hang-ups (mainly to do with tradition and a bit of denominationalism), but adding good works to the condition for salvation is not one of them. Salvation is truly a gift of God, not of works. Lutheran Christians are certain of that.

(May I tell one quick story? We were building a gymnasium and six additional classrooms with volunteer labor. God, as He characteristically does, put in place a great guy with the gift of administration. He co-ordinated the work of the volunteers with the work of the contractor, the volunteers usually working Monday and Thursday evenings and also on Saturdays. One evening, only a handful of volunteers was there. One of the guys was chairman of the school board at that time. He had been raised in a denomi-nation that is known for emphasizing the addition of good works, rather than "grace alone" for salvation. On this occasion this guy said, "Pastor, I know we Lutherans teach salvation by grace alone, but tonight it seems like adding works wouldn't hurt!" He knew, of course, that this was meant to be humorous.)

Four: Speaking of not helping with our salvation, 1 Corinthians 12:3 makes it abundantly clear that even coming to faith we do not do on our own, but God gives the Holy Spirit so that we can say, "Jesus is Lord." "Jesus is Lord" is simply the first of Christian creeds. If one is a Christian, one states, "Jesus is Lord." Of course, He is many other things as well, specifically, "Savior," which is here implied. This verse is important to help us understand how very interested God is in our lives, to the point of making sure we have a relationship with Him.

Five: Romans 8:38-39 is what is needed to give us the confidence that once we are in Christ (faith relationship), nothing can separate us from Him. I would read this at virtually every funeral/memorial service. Actually, I got to the point that I didn't care if I used the same Scripture verses every time, for like this one, they are so meaningful. Nothing, that's nothing, can separate us from the love of God—which love?—the love of God that is in Christ Jesus our Lord! Wonderful!

And what does Paul list? First of all neither death nor life. You see for the Christian, it matters not if the relationship we have with Christ continues here on earth or there in heaven. The body may die (see verse 8), but the soul, that is the spirit, mind, and personality, continues living—that's why there's no separation. Paul also lists some things that one might think could negatively affect our secure relationship, *viz.* demons, things that are going on in our lives now, things to come in the future. They simply cannot and they will not take us from the love of God in Christ. Important concept. Important verse.

The Second Five

If you only know five more verses of the Bible, which should those be?

Six: Romans 10:9 sums it up so nicely. Want to be saved? Confess the original creed, "Jesus is Lord," and believe in your heart—that is your very most important self that God raised Jesus from the dead. No resurrection, no salvation. No atoning sacrifice, still in our sins. But . . . Jesus is raised from the dead—believing that (by the power of the Holy Spirit—see verse 4) with your most-inner self is what saves. Then say it! This all goes together so nicely!

Seven: If there's one verse in the Bible that assures us that, regardless of how it looks, God is working, it's Romans 8:28. This verse is so encouraging, so assuring. God is working for good for those who love Him—those who have a personal relationship with Him through Christ. We have been called. And . . . God does have a purpose for our lives. Regardless of what happens, God can use it for good. And He does.

Eight: Lazarus died. Both Mary and Martha expressed their disappointment that Jesus hadn't been there. Their friends wondered that Jesus hadn't prevented this death. Jesus used the occasion as a teaching opportunity. It is of vast interest to me that during the years following my memorization of this passage, I figured out what was being said. I previously thought Jesus simply repeated the thought. In fact, I had wondered on occasion why He said it twice. I thought probably for emphasis. However, I now understand that indeed this is great comfort for survivors at the time of a death.

Family members and friends go to the viewing, they go to the funeral, they go to the cemetery, they witness the obvious lack of life in the body. But that is only part of what has happened. The body, indeed has died, but Jesus promises that it will live again. "He who believes in me, though he die, yet shall he live." That very dead body will live again and be made very new as it is reunited with the rest of the person. Jesus' second statement speaks to that.

". . . and whoever lives and believes in me will never die." (John 11:25-26) The person sure looks dead in the casket, but that's just the body. The soul did not die (see the chapter on the 5th commandment and the comment "he's not here anymore"). So . . . what's living? What didn't die? Everything of the person that is not physical. This includes the mind, the spirit, the personality, the emotions—all of what we know about ourselves that is not body, never dies! The person simply goes to be with the Lord.

Then what about the body in heaven? It's clear that those who die in the Lord have two different existences in heaven. They are there before the rapture (second coming of Christ), and they are united with their bodies when Christ comes again. 1 Thessalonians 4:14&16, "We believe that Jesus died and rose again and so we believe that God will bring with Jesus those who have fallen asleep in him [that is their souls] . . . For the Lord himself will come down from heaven, with a loud command, with the voice of the arch-angel and with the trumpet call of God, and the dead in Christ [their bodies] will rise first." Wow!

By the way, it is frequently asked if we will know our loved ones in heaven. That question is so clearly answered in the account of the Transfiguration. It was obvious that those appearing from heaven were Moses and Elijah. No doubt about it!

Nine: When Jesus was asked which was the greatest of the com-mandments He answered clearly in Matthew 22:37-39, that loving God is number one and just like it loving neighbor as self is number two. What Jesus said that day was that the Ten commandments can be summed up and understood with loving God (1-3), and loving others (4-10). This, then, is the expectation of how to live—loving

God and others as fully as we possibly can. But wait—there's more!

In Matthew 22 Jesus summed up the Old Testament Law in a very real way, but at the last supper, the night before He died, He gave new understanding, in fact, He gave a new commandment that blended the two and described Christian witness to the world. John 13:34, "A new command I give you: Love one another. As I have loved you, so you must love one another. By this all will know that you are my disciples, if you love one another." Filled with the Holy Spirit, when followers of Jesus are loved, so is God! This is no longer a commandment to keep God's Law, but now is a commandment to demonstrate God's salvation in our lives.

Loving one another (in the Body of Christ) is the model of behavior we should have in the Church. Loving one another is the demonstration to the world that we are experiencing God's love in our lives because of our faith relationship with Him.

Ten: Now a verse that is of major encouragement to us as followers of Jesus Christ. This passage has everything to do with Christian living. And as such, it has a great deal to do with our personal spiritual, psychological and emotional well being. Philippians 4:4-7. So what does it tell us? Rejoice, display gentleness, no angst, pray and give thanks, and experience peace.

Rejoice in the Lord always. Always? Well, I'm not always happy. There are things in my life that are not good—sometimes very negative. They are brought on by circumstances. They are brought on by others. They are brought on by me. They make me not very happy. Paul's counsel? Rejoice! Joy, you see, is different from happiness. Joy comes from the Lord, from our relationship with God through Jesus Christ. It can be, and actually is, there regardless of what and regardless of whom. It also needs to be expressed regardless of me! So rejoice—experience the joy of your relationship with God.

"Let your gentleness be evident to all." Now, dear Paul, you are meddling! I don't always want to do that. In fact, there are those who would say I am not gentle. So . . . take a look. If, indeed God loves me intensely, and He does, might I not live my life for others? Indeed, see verse 9. Living for God and others simply means putting myself aside, including emotional action that is not gentle. In this way our gentleness is exhibited and love is perceived. "By this all will know you are my disciples, if you have love for one another."

No anxiety. I include here worry. People, including Christians, have a tendency to worry. I have come up with my "worry formula," and I am committed to it enough to have shared it from the pulpit, not that I've actually been in the pulpit for some time (see chapter including Dave Anderson). I've suggested to the congregation if they must worry, let them take ten minutes a day to worry. They can even make a list, if they wish, to remind them of all the things they'd like to worry about. Then, during those ten minutes (once a day only), they can worry about all these things. At the end of the ten minutes, they are to say a prayer, giving all these things over to the Lord. Then, when they are tempted to worry about something later in the day, they are to remind themselves that this has been given over to the Lord, and they have no need to worry about it any longer (maybe in the worry minutes tomorrow, but not today!).

I was making a hospital call towards the end of the afternoon. The woman I was visiting asked me if I worked all the time. I said, "No. Five to seven every day belongs to my family. I'm always at home." She said, "With all the responsibilities of a pastor, how do you accomplish that?" I simply told her that at 5 o'clock I turn it all over to the Lord and I trust Him to take care of it.

(As long as I broached this subject, I'd like to share my thoughts on the pastor's work week. Since pastors have responsibilities on

Sunday, my Sabbath was on Monday. No "just checking on one thing." No phone calls. No contact (obviously emergencies are honored—see chapter including Dora, which happened on a Monday). I always joked (except I wasn't joking), that if I saw a parishioner in a store on Monday, I would make sure to go down another aisle. Any time a pastor is with one of the members, he's at work! Really! I tried to work 55 hours a week. I figured that many salaried people worked 50 hours a week and then volunteered at church, so I would give my extra five hours as well.)

Now . . . in my opinion, the next counsel from Paul is one of the great keys to Christian living. In everything, thanksgiving. I believe that this literally means thanking God for *whatever* is going on. I truly mean that. It has never failed me to thank God for every and any situation. I do remember once thinking, "I just can't do that this time." But I did. Now I don't remember what it was. What I do know, is that your Christian life will be blessed and your emotional life will be better, if indeed you thank God always.

And finally the promise, "And the peace of God, which transcends all understanding, will guard your hearts and your minds in Christ Jesus." Inner peace comes from God. The promise is that His peace will guard our hearts (spirit, emotions, personality) and our minds (thinking) so that we will be at ease and ready to serve God and others. What a joy. What a blessing!

Know what's in these verses and apply them to your life. It makes a major difference!

Chapter Thirteen

Using Gifts, Producing Fruit
≈

I was in the first few years of pastoring when I had the opportunity to go to a Spiritual Gifts Seminar. I sat there fascinated,
wondering why I had never before heard of this approach to spiritual gifts. In fact, while the Bible passages were familiar to me, the
teaching of how spiritual gifts were given and used, was not.

The teacher listed over 20 spiritual gifts, teaching that they
were given to Christians for a specific purpose. Scripture is quite
clear that God chooses who will have which gift(s), and that they
are to be used to conduct the mission and ministry of the Church
(Body of Christ), and the church (local congregation). Again—I sat
fascinated.

This chapter cannot possibly be a "Spiritual Gifts Workshop,"
but I'd just like to highlight a few things:

- "Each one should use whatever gift he has received to serve
  others, faithfully administering God's grace in its various
  forms." (1 Peter 4:10 NIV)
- "Now to each one the manifestation of the Spirit is
  given for the common good." (1 Corinthians 12:7) ".
  . . so that the body of Christ may be built up . . ."
  (Ephesians 4:12 NIV)
- "But to each one of us grace has been given as Christ

apportioned it...to prepare God's people for works of service."
(Ephesians 4:7&12)

The result of all this is a well-functioning church in which the
fruit of the Spirit is enjoyed by individual Christians and by the
congregation. While the gifts are distributed among the people,
everyone having one or more, but not all, the fruit of the Spirit is
for everyone. All are to experience love, joy, peace, patience, kind-
ness, goodness, gentleness, faithfulness and self-control as stated in
Galatians 5:22-23. The gifts are given that the fruit might be produced. Everyone needs to use his or her gift.

And when they are used, the church thrives and members experience a great deal of satisfaction using their gifts. It is the astute
congregation that recognizes this and gives opportunity to its members to use their spiritual gifts. This is so much better than asking
people to perform ministry for which they have not been gifted.

How do you know? There are several great spiritual gift workshop models out there. The most challenging part is getting the
current members to participate. Easier is having new members
take a spiritual gifts inventory as part of new member orientation.
Important is having spiritual gift categories as fields in the church's
computer. Really. Then . . . when pastoral or lay leadership needs
to ask for something to be done, the computer person runs a list of
the requested gift (e.g. teaching, administration, hospitality, evangelism, mercy), and the right people can be asked!

When I teach a spiritual gifts workshop, I have example after
example of people who blessed the congregation by using their spiritual gifts. Every congregation has the gifts necessary to carry out
the ministry God wants done.

I'm only going to comment on one particular gift, because
knowing this and putting it into practice can save a lot of grief in a

congregation, and actually get a lot more done. This is the spiritual gift of leadership (Romans 12:8). It is imperative that those with the spiritual gift of leadership work together and that they work with the pastor, who may or may not have the gift of leadership. Having more than one person trying to lead a congregation in different ways is not God pleasing and it is chaotic.

This chapter could be a lot longer, but I simply encourage you to check this out and do a study on spiritual gifts.

Well, it seems that this is the end. Actually it ended at a good place, for if a congregation identifies and puts to use the spiritual gifts that God has already given them, people will be blessed and ministry will happen. So . . . if you have the gift of leadership, get on it—find someone with the gift of administration to get it organized, and pray that the pastor is on board! God bless you.

EPILOGUE

Having just read through the manuscript for *Views from the Pulpit* one more time, I noticed how very autobiographical this is. I didn't mean it to be about me, but about the experiences of being a pastor. On second thought, however, it occurs to me that a story about God's work (history—His Story) is the way He works in people's lives. This book is about how He has worked in my life.

The Good News of salvation through our Savior and Lord Jesus is that it always is a working in the life of an individual. His Story is also lived out in your life and you are the one to tell your observations of God working, just as I have told mine.

God bless us all to that end!

CPSIA information can be obtained at www.ICGtesting.com
Printed in the USA
BVOW031943151012

303057BV00003B/121/P